LETTERS TO

Also from Carcanet

Under Storm's Wing
Helen Thomas
with Myfanwy Thomas

Letters to Helen

EDWARD THOMAS

**and an appendix of seven letters to
Harry and Janet Hooton**

Edited by

R. GEORGE THOMAS

with a foreword by Myfanwy Thomas

CARCANET

First published in Great Britain in 2000 by
Carcanet Press Limited
4th Floor, Conavon Court
12–16 Blackfriars Street
Manchester M3 5BQ

A CIP catalogue record for this book is available from the British Library.
ISBN 1 85754 447 1

The publisher acknowledges financial assistance from
the Arts Council of England.

Set in Monotype Bell by XL Publishing Services, Tiverton
Printed and bound in England by SRP Ltd, Exeter

Contents

R.A. MESS,
TINTOWN,
LYDD.

14 Jii 16

Kuest, my letter came at last —
some time yesterday, & soon after it
(by the way) a cheque book from Cox's
bank.

Well now I don't know
what to say. I fully hope to reach
home some time Saturday night with
at least 24 hours' leave. But I
might have to go straight to
Aldershot without time to see
you. If so I will wire when
I know, which I expect will be
when the list is read out on
Saturday morning — telling us
our places in the Exam. and
the batteries we go to. My

Foreword

Having read and re-read these letters – often poignant, often sad or disturbing, sometimes full of lively fun – between our parents from their early courting days to their parting, it is impossible for me to make a sensible, unemotional comment. Mother told us that as a girl in her early teens her proudest moment was when her beloved father, James Ashcroft Noble, told her, 'Nellie, you are the queen of letter writers'. In these letters her energy, warmth and courage are felt even when she is desolated; in Edward's, truth and honesty about everything he thinks and feels. Combined, these qualities are indestructible.

It was a pleasure to be asked if I would like to write a family note about this selection of letters. For the child who sent a hundred loves to her father in France with the last letter of Helen's to reach him, is now a great-grandmother to Helen and Rachel. But on re-reading these letters, I find that George Thomas has introduced them with such knowledge and understanding, there is nothing I want to add.

Mother, after her first long meeting with R.G.T., was bright-eyed and happily amazed at how well the Cardiff professor *knew* and understood the complexity of Edward's nature. She was overjoyed and buoyant, knowing he was the man she could trust to write about her husband. Perhaps it was the two men's Welshness which made for this understanding, for I am sure that my father's feeling of searching for something, of not belonging, came from a yearning – *hiraeth* (a beautiful, untranslatable Welsh word) – to belong to Wales, but that he could not honestly ease his way in, as it were, without being born and reared there.

So now, speaking for our family and friends, I offer our warmest thanks and deep appreciation to a devoted editor and biographer, a True Thomas indeed, for all he has done for our parents and their work.

MYFANWY THOMAS

Introduction

These letters are chosen from over a thousand exchanged between Edward and Helen Thomas during their twenty-one years together, 642 letters dating from the first six years of their courtship and early marriage. The remainder record the occasions (in 1903, 1908, 1911, 1913) when Edward felt impelled to leave home and stay as a paying guest with family or friends, either to find extra literary journalism in London or to secure a calm place of friendly, if isolated, retreat from domestic bustle and petty worries. Especially after late 1910, he fought hard with himself to write books that corresponded more closely to the inner promptings of his response to experience. In January 1913 he contributed his view on 'How I Began' to a series in *T.P.'s Weekly*. At this time his doubts were legion about the 'success' of his numerous books, essays, reviews and articles. His invitation to contribute to the series, and his emergence as a significant critic of the 'new' Georgian poetry, indicate his real stature among fellow writers. This article is a short, incisive pointer to the subterranean direction of his wrestle with words which – twenty-one months later – produced his first remarkable poems: 'Up in the Wind', 'November Sky', 'March', 'Old Man', 'The Signpost', and 'The Other'.

'How I Began' states explicitly the close relationship between his familiar letters and his destined direction as a writer:

While I was afflicted with serious English composition and English literature, I was reading Scott, Fenimore Cooper, Henty, and the travellers, because I loved them; I was also thinking and talking in a manner which owed little to those dignified exercises, though the day was to come when I spoke very much as I wrote. Presently, also, myself and English as she is taught in schools, came to a conflict, and gradually to a more and more friendly agreement through the necessity of writing long letters daily to one who was neither a schoolboy nor an elder, the subject of the letters being matters concerning nobody else in the world. Now it was that I had a chance of discarding or adapting to my own purpose the fine words and infinite variety of constructions which I had formerly admired from afar off and imitated in fairly cold blood. There is no doubt that my masters often lent me dignity and subtlety altogether beyond my needs.

Both in these letters and in papers intended for print, I ravaged the language (to the best of my ability) at least as much for ostentation as for use, though I should not like to have to separate the two.

This last sentence is a shrewd comment on the varied quality of his rapidly written prose works. Yet, more significant for me was the caveat that his letters to Helen were on 'matters concerning nobody else in the world'. In obedience – without comment on the fact that this correspondence has been faithfully preserved (initially, I suspect, by Edward) – I have severely restricted my selection from the 642 letters that passed between them from 1896 to 1900.

Thereafter their letters centred around Edward's long absences from home. Absences caused by his occasionally severe, but not incapacitating, bouts of depression (then termed 'neurasthenia'), by his obsessive concern with sufficient income to provide for his children's education, for the provision of a peaceful, unostentatious rural home for his family, and, less obviously, by his demand for personal freedom to test fully his response to his 'kingdoms three': 'The lovely visible earth and sky and sea'. This was a solitary quest,

And it would be the same were no house near.
Over all sorts of weather, men, and times,
Aspens must shake their leaves and men may hear
But need not listen, more than to my rhymes.

This private quest was as relentlessly pursued as his later embrace of military duty in France. It was tempered by his growing awareness of another call on himself, best articulated in the probing poem 'Wind and Mist':

There were whole days and nights when the wind and I
Between us shared the world, and the wind ruled
And I obeyed it and forgot the mist.
My past and the past of the world were in the wind.
Now you will say that though you understand
And feel for me, and so on, you yourself
Would find it different. You are all like that
If once you stand here free from wind and mist:
I might as well be talking to wind and mist.
You would believe the house-agent's young man
Who gives no heed to anything I say.
Good morning. But one word. I want to admit
That I would try the house once more, if I could;
As I should like to try being young again.

This is the authentic voice that I have found in all the post-Oxford letters of Edward Thomas, clearly balanced by Helen's sensitive approach to practical day-to-day affairs, constantly guided by his counsel and requests.

Slick generalisations have no place in any posthumous attempt to assess the strengths and weaknesses of the tensile qualities that sustained a marriage between two differently gifted people, drawn together by passionate physical attraction and an equally powerful determination to respect each other's free development, the one as a creative writer, the other as a homemaker. Certainly at Elses Farm, The Weald (1904–6), Berryfield Cottage, Ashford (1906–9), Wick Green, Froxfield (1910–13) and Yew Tree Cottage, Steep (1914–15), Edward enjoyed longish periods of profitable writing. They were seasoned by the frequent weekend visits of many writers and family friends and his own regular fortnightly appearances at London literary luncheon gatherings. His final return to Steep was marked by a £100 award from the Royal Literary Fund, his rapid friendship with Robert Frost, the onset of war, his subsequent enlistment in July 1915, and the outrush of his poetry, 85 of his 144 poems being written in eight months. This last year and a half in Steep saw the return of that unblinkered yet passionate 'friendship' which their earliest courtship days had promised. Edward's 73 letters to Helen from France, like his 71 letters during his first long stay in London in 1903–4, give substance to Helen's vivid recall, in *World Without End*, of their last night together in January 1917: 'So we lay, all night, sometimes talking of our love and all that had been, and of the children, and what had been amiss and what right. We knew the best was that there had never been untruth between us. We knew all of each other, and it was right.'

This sense of balanced amity is echoed in his letter in March 1916 when Helen first read his frank poem about his father (*P.H.T.*):

Dearest, Fancy your thinking those verses had anything to do with you. Fancy your thinking, too, that I should let you see them if they were. They are not to a woman at all. You know precisely all that I know of any woman I have cared a little for: they are as a matter of fact to father. So now, unless you choose to think I am deceiving you (which I don't think I ever did), you can be at ease again. Silly old thing to jump so to conclusions. You might as well have concluded the verses to Mother (*M.E.T.*) were for you. As to the other verses about love you know that my usual belief is that I don't and can't love and haven't done for something near 20 years. You know too that you don't think my nature really compatible with love, being so clear and critical. You know how unlike I am to you, and you know that you love, so how can I? That is if you count love as any one feeling and not something varying infinitely with the variety of people.

These two poems were the first in the group he called his 'Household Poems', ending with the truth-ridden poem to Helen, 'And you, Helen, what should I give you?' with its haunting conclusion:

I would give you back yourself
And power to discriminate
What you want and want it not too late,

Many fair days free from care
And heart to enjoy both foul and fair.
And myself, too, if I could find
Where it lay hidden and it proved kind.

Helen's letters, like her books, speak as clearly and effectively as she spoke to me in the last years of her long, fruitful life. Her last thirty years were spent in the country, sustained by a firm, unsentimental belief that this was how she and Edward would have ended their days together. As their daily, twenty-five-to-thirty-pages-long courtship letters show, their instant friendship developed around exploratory walks on South London commons. Helen was a willing pupil and she built on this acquired love of Nature for the rest of her life, beginning with walks with five-months old Merfyn across Clapham Common and the railway embankment on Wandsworth Common:

> In this place which I had begun to feel was quite barren, we are discovering all sorts of treasures and Merfyn is as pleased as I. But we long for the country, where we shall not only look at roses and lotus through an iron fence, but touch them... My longing for the country has become a passion.

And years after this first walk in June 1900, she could still interweave her love of flowers with her continuing love of Edward:

> White Bryony and stitchwort have become to me almost symbolic. If I could make a mystic picture of my spiritual life since I first loved you, it would have a garland of these two flowers about it. I remember days on Wimbledon common when you were away, how I searched for White Byrony and was joyous having found it – though I never picked it – feeling sure of your love then – I don't know why. And so it lingers now, and I like to see Merfyn with it about his dear old head. (8 June 1907)

From the beginning, her intensely passionate love was tested against his frequent absences: she never found them easy to accept and repeatedly explained her deepest feelings with a candour based on the honesty of their mutual friendship. When Edward first visited Gordon Bottomley at Cartmel near Windermere in June 1907, she felt he was as far 'as if you were at the North Pole':

for everything is so different: the country, the people, the house, the ways, the thoughts. Everything is unlike home, and this must seem very far away and dim to you. Oh I wish it could be always as pleasant to you to be here, as it seems it would be now: for I guess that because of the kind of house you are in, the people, the quiet beautiful orderly life, that all makes a mist between you and home, and you see it as one sees the moor sometimes with a golden halo. Perhaps it is not so with you. I try so hard to know your thoughts, your feelings about things. Pleasure comes because my love fills me so in every part of me; yet sweet though it is, it is so little really for all that it means to me. It is over so soon; but often when I cry out with my lips and my breast and my limbs, I wish my love might be free to find some other way that you might know it, and be glad just as you are when we lie together.

There were to be further times of absence and stress. They were fuelled by a constant struggle with his nervous temperament and fed by a deep disappointment that, although he could meet his own financial expectations, there was no ready critical understanding of the direction his work was taking. He was 'religious' but without a creed. Curiously, as all his careful diaries show, he had always imposed a strict pattern on each long working day. He balanced reading, writing, and exercise; he recorded the precise word-counts for his articles, reviews, stories, essays and books; he maintained a running account of all items of income and expenditure. Away from home he maintained the same working habits (and their records) like a protective cocoon, and despite periods of despair – never alleviated by a variety of doctors – he scrupulously met his many deadlines with editors and publishers. At such times, because he had opened his heart (and mind) before her in tumultuous courtship letters, Helen was prepared to wait patiently until he could find the way to a true sense of purpose, accompanied by peace of mind. Although she was proud and amazed at the ferocity he brought to his soldiering, Helen tempered hope that he would survive with a thinly disguised conviction that he would not return from France. For her, his poetry – and the subsequent slow yet increasing critical acclaim it received – was a major tribute to their up-and-down life together. She agreed at once to my suggestion that a broadcast interview-talk we had prepared should be called 'True Thomas'. (It never was.)

The honesty of their love and friendship, I believe, shines through this short selection, although their letters reflect initially their days apart. For a half-century after his death, Helen was sustained by the double evidence that they 'had come through' and so realised the high hopes of their courtship years: the first was the poetry, which she had always believed was his natural medium; the other was the shared war-time experience of his seventy-three letters to her. Those letters balance detailed observation – which he hoped could be used in his post-war writing – with small personal touches of assurance and self-revelation. On 17 March 1917, after a detailed description of a walk to his Observation Post through a bombed suburb that earlier had been No Man's Land, he concludes:

> My dearest, if it weren't for these things I shouldn't be really alive. Actually now I hear a lark singing above the street as well as the slops splashing out. And you must not convince yourself that you are merely waiting, you know. You must have been content or happy at Ivy's [Ransome], if you come to think of it, and however well life goes on in war or peace, one doesn't get more than that, though of course I know you want more and so do I.

On the first of April, after a full account of twenty-four hours observing German positions in the new Front Line, he again involves Helen's activities in his own:

> You are having a fine Easter, I hope, as we are, though not a

warm one yet. I like hearing of your days with Baba and Bronwen and Joy, and of Mervyn's ride with Ernest, and intended ride to Jesse's. But here is Rubin saying he gets bored stiff if he is alone. Never mind. I liked hearing about your bath, too, and your working and the children eating. Rubin has set the gramophone to 'In Cellar cool'. But everything, gramophone or not, out here forbids memories such as you have been writing. Memories I have but they are mixed up with my thoughts and feelings in Beaurains or when I hear the blackbirds or when the old dog bangs the table leg with his tail or lies with his brains wasting in his skull. You must not therefore expect me to say anything outright. It is not my way, is it?

The 1038 letters from which this selection was made were preserved by Helen and, I believe, informed her two books, *As It Was* and *World Without End* with a feeling of sensitive authenticity, although these were written some years after his death, almost as therapy against a delayed severe breakdown. Her first response to his death, and the end of all her hopes, was a letter to him under the heading *April 9 to June 1917*. It is in a commonplace notebook begun in late 1914, with Helen's fair copy of the early poems entitled 'November' and 'March'. It is included as a poignant postscript to all their familiar letters.

In France, Edward read some of Shakespeare's sonnets last thing at night. His final unfinished poem survives partially in Helen's copy and wholly on the last page of the diary he kept in France. Probably written on 13 January at Lydd, before embarkation, it is the third of another set of 'household poems' along with 'The Lane' (their last walk together in Froxfield) and 'Out in the Dark' (a Christmas Eve poem) about their last home in High Beech, near Loughton. With his usual honesty, this last poem for Helen, set down without extenuation, is a natural outcome of all their life together:

The sorrow of true love is a great sorrow
And true love parting blackens a bright morrow:
Yet almost they equal joys, since their despair

Is but hope blinded by its tears, and clear
Above the storm the heavens wait to be seen.
But greater sorrow from less love has been
That can mistake lack of despair for hope
And knows not tempest and the perfect scope
Of summer, but a frozen drizzle perpetual
Of drops that from remorse and pity fall
And cannot ever shine in the sun or thaw,
Removed eternally from the sun's law.

'Last Poem' belongs as much to their familiar letters as to his
Collected Poems: it records a shared experience that held firm
against all the odds.

R. George Thomas
Llanishen, Cardiff

Editorial Note

The text of these letters was edited from the original manuscripts in the National Library of Wales, Aberystwyth (NLW) and the Edward Thomas Collection in the Humanities Library of the University of Wales, Cardiff (ETC). The edition was made possible by the kind permission of the poet's daughter, Myfanwy Thomas, and the devoted co-operation of the two Librarians and their staff, especially Daniel Huws and Brian Ll. James, who have helped me at all times beyond the call of duty.

John Moore, the original biographer of Edward Thomas, quoted parts of the letters from France in his *Life and Letters of Edward Thomas*, but with many occasional omissions. I have quoted one letter in my Writers of Wales monograph (*Edward Thomas*) and another in *Edward Thomas: A Portrait*. This is the first time, however, that these letters have been edited within the context of the 1042 letters between Edward and Helen that have survived. Readers who wish to follow up the brief footnotes to the text should find necessary information in the short *Further Reading* list.

R.G.T.

Further Reading

Books by Edward Thomas:
Horae Solitariae, 1902
Rose Acre Papers, 1904
Feminine Influence on the Poets, 1910
Rest and Unrest, 1910
The Happy-Go-Lucky Morgans, 1913 (strongly autobiographical)
In Pursuit of Spring, 1914
The Childhood of Edward Thomas, with a Preface by Julian
  Thomas, 1938; with a Preface by Roland Gant, 1983
Collected Poems, edited by R. George Thomas (Oxford: Clarendon
  Press), 1978
Selected Letters, edited by R. George Thomas (Oxford University
  Press), 1995

Others:
Helen Thomas, *Time and Again*, edited by Myfanwy Thomas
  (Manchester: Carcanet Press), 1978
Myfanwy Thomas, *One of these fine days*, memoirs (Manchester:
  Carcanet Press), 1982
Helen Thomas with Myfanwy Thomas, *Under Storm's Wing*
  (Manchester: Carcanet Press), 1988; 1997
R. George Thomas, *Edward Thomas. A Portrait* (Oxford:
  Clarendon Press), 1985

1: *To Helen*

My dearest friend,[1]

Everyday when late sleeping does not prevent me I rise at half past six and go out for an hour or nearly; then breakfast; read a little for the ten o'clock post; then go out again: in the afternoon I take a third walk, usually a fourth in the evening at sunset. And, is it the strangest part of this system, that my walks are absolutely without any variety, at least of scene? First, I go alongside the canal, between a tall thorn hedge and ranks of flag and meadowsweet and parsley that grow at the edge of the water. The bryony is in the hedge, quite near: already it is covered in green flower; a few berries cluster among the leaves: the stems knit all the thorns together with their pliant paleness: and I take a quiet pleasure in looking at the cool fair leaves, the tendrils, and the humid bines. This same quiet pleasure of perfect content is what characterises all my walks. I cultivate it: I find it almost an ideal state: it falls short of the ideal in being, not too dispassionate, but too conscious, although its merit is that it is nevertheless extremely self-unconscious. I walk slowly and with downward eyes, almost without a thought; looking at the curve of the stately reeds which is like the poise of the old Gods; or seeing the ferny hill lose itself among white clouds; or following the branching of the meadowsweet. Only I often sigh, quite involuntarily, though sometimes I can explain it; and these occasions (when I can explain) are when I realise the imperfection of my mood, and how much it lacks of reverence; which is the unhappiest result of having formed a sort of theory of perfect behaviour in such scenes. I enjoy the songs of birds at times, but not often: I never could enjoy them much, though doubtless they have combined with other things to cause my delights: perhaps my surroundings are too imperfect for it; but more likely I am incapable of it, and terriblest of all I am so miserably conscious of myself that I even think of how I could describe it, actually while I gaze! how mean! how ridiculous! what prose fancy! In fact, generally in my relations with Nature I feel very much like that man of whom Rousseau tells that he left his mistress to write of her. But my action is almost incomparable for meanness, and so ludicrous. Yet here are times, however few, when it is Nature is too strong and I am forced into my place, am humble, reverent, pious; how thankful I am for these few occasions. With you sometimes in the wild wood, sweet-heart, I feel that my mien and behaviour are nearly perfect; but too constrained, too limited by my physical weakness and instability, too broken now and then also by conscience reminding of little but necessary performances, for perfection. I think you, Helen, must feel almost perfectly pious in these hours; not quite, because the restraint which causes (does it?) a feeling of meanness, if not grotesqueness, at times. But I think you differ from me in your actual attitude – even in the attitude you seek and think ideal, towards Nature; though just how I can not define. Am I, or am I not, entirely stupid and reprehensible in my fashioning of a sort of ideal reverence towards Nature and writing it down as I do directly or indirectly in all my work? I sometimes think all this my religion might be written by everyone on the basis of Shelley's *Alastor* and *Mont Blanc*, Keats' Odes and *Hyperion*, Victor Hugo (a little, very little), and Jefferies (less still); along with pieces from Ruskin and many others; recollections, too, of Matthew Arnold's 'Youth and Nature' or something like it ('We, O Nature, depart, Thou survivest us –'). And I have got to find whence I adopted my affectation of admiration, if not love, of the spirit of children: I expect it is nothing very wonderful, yet I can not credit even that much as original. I don't think I owe anything to Virgil and Horace, and though I often imitate their expressions, it is a pedantic, superficial, imitation, and not one of the spirit, – I expect.

My walk is almost entirely along the canal-bank, which becomes pleasanter continually as I leave the town; the hedge is taller, the weeds at the brim are denser; the water too is somewhat purer and clearer, and the sandmartins more frequent. Running *under the canal*, as you know, sweet heart, is the willowed brook (where does 'wild and willowed shore' come from?) where the watervoles go through parted reeds and flowers: but only today, though it lies under my path, did I first visit the place. In truth, loathing is mingled with my liking for it: since of late years I believe they have turned a sewer into the water and dulled its ripples, killed its trout, and spoiled the sweetness of its cresses

2

and its reeds. But I was enchanted with it today. It is the densest thicket of thorn and hemlock and sweet tall-grass and flowers that I know; the one willow shades most of it, and young ash trees lean their tender branches over the rest; there are red robins here, and ragged robins, and in the brook the fair flags and the flagflowers and sedge where the birds creep; in the willows I see the bullfinch and its young, or the little berry-brown young wrens by scores among the leaves. It is not a perfectly sweet (I use *sweet* in a permitted sense – health, vitality, ardour are implied) place, but still the thick perfume of so many leaves and stems and swards overcomes disgust, and the brook indeed is bright enough and transparent, although I fear that we two shall never bathe our weariness there as I used to long ago, – in the young years, when, in spite of everything, I was purer because really ingenuous and not as now only contriving ingenuousness and recognising it as an ideal. Still, though we can not cool ourselves among the reed tufts, where the birds bathe yet, we shall lie and rove here many times, Helen, beautiful one.

Sad, too, it is, that I usually take a book with me, – Keats or Virgil. O, the Odes of Keats! and Isabella! and Hyperion! I am full of them; Isabella in its way is perfect; the Odes, also, (Grecian Urn, Melancholy, Autumn especially) are perfect. And by the way, do you know Keats' 'Robin Hood'? O, read it; there are charming pieces in it:

Gone the song of Gamelyn, Gone the merry morris din,
Gone the tough belted outlaw, Idling in the 'grené shaw'.

I am afraid my enthusiasm about the Odes appears very windy since I do not explain; but, beyond recommending them to your love, I have no time; some day, when I return, I will certainly talk of them; only do not think I am become drunk over them, with a windy sentimental delight (*remember what I read by Matthew Arnold on Keats*).

I don't read Rousseau out of doors, but I read it rapidly indoors. You ought to read it; only do not, in translation. Reflect on this, in these good days, when we are shocked (like Mrs Noble) at the name of Rousseau, that he lay with no woman until he was twenty two, and then only with her whom he loved most in the

3

world and with whom the boon was most priceless. But Madame de Warlus had been persuaded by a lover when young into a belief that sexual connection was a small matter, like shaking hands; and this unhappy sophism had the effect of making her ready (purely, it would seem) to concede this pleasure to almost any man. I will tell you all when we talk together; but I fear that I have raised a difficult surmise in your mind?

I hope you are happy now, that you have been, and that this letter has not upset your happiness, my own sweet little one. You were happy when you wrote last, and O, surely you are still happy; I cannot be even content when you are unhappy, which is not often as it is with me. So you will tell me.

I wonder does this letter appear no more than the product of my brain? In truth, I do seem to live more upon my brain now. It needs your presence to make me dare to feel passion. Yet, as I have repeated, I am nonetheless [more] moved towards you, little one, than when I wrote such wild letters, apparently full of imaginative passion, but in which disease and Shelley entered largely. I can never satisfy my passion, nor approach its satisfying, except actually in your arms, little one. I am aloof, and cold, and embarrassed at other times; and partly then, because of its incompleteness, and the restraint even upon its incompleteness.

How short a letter, and when letters are so rare for you! none the less you will not leave me with so few, so short letters, will you? And in truth mine seems too long; just news that I am alive is all of worth, and yet both in you and in me such as this even gives some satisfaction. Tell me if it fails; oh, but it cannot, sweetheart. Goodbye, my own sweet little one, let me kiss your brow as we go in the cool dusk; or we will lie together and dream over the barrier, poor sweet one. Goodbye. I am in life your truest, fondest friend, Edward, and you are still and forever my own sweet little one, Helen, my anemone maiden. Goodbye. Do you sleep happy, and are you well?

NLW

1 ET had made Helen Noble's acquaintance in 1895; both her mother (now widowed) and his parents wished to restrict their friendship at this stage. ET was preparing to go up to Oxford, and Helen had a variety of jobs, with spells at home.

2: *To Helen*

My dearest friend,

It has been rainy weather for several days now, and we are kept indoors mostly; on Friday – yesterday, for example – we were not able to go to Llandilo, Gwili and I, as we intended.[1] Yet the confinement is full of pleasures. If only I heard more often and more profusely from you, I could almost be content. The ignorance, good nature, comfortable wealth, and health, of the place are very lulling, and, as I said, for one so conceited and affected as myself, very flattering. Nevertheless, – and this as well, – I am not satisfied with myself; such idleness, such selfishness, is not a desirable life; all this flattery is certainly no good atmosphere for me. I fret under it, fortunately. I am a craven soul, and yet I see that this life is too mean. Very small convenience is enough for me to work in, as you know, – a chair and a table – and a window. But I must also have a room that is *lived in*, constantly; and here only the kitchen, where we dine and cook, is the only frequented room. It is here therefore that I choose to work, not in the sittingroom encumbered with trumpery and abundant decorations. So here I sit, and of course do no satisfactory work, only scraps, whether it be classics, history or literature or writing; for sometimes I laugh and talk with the rest (whoever happens to be in), and in any case I am bound to listen. I am perpetually in a soaking mood as when one listens to a barrel organ and opens the mouth (in ecstasy): nothing I do is well done – why! I am fain to endeavour even now to put some artistic care in my writing to you; but I can't. It is too plebeian. I believe I am plebeian myself, believe also that I was meant not to be plebeian; yet I shall never be anything more. Nevertheless I maintain a sort of rebellion against sinking into the filth of the democracy, that breed, eat, like pigs. Not but that I still dwell affectionately upon the simplicity and sincerity of these people, though I have found that even such a tiny village contains adultery, illegitimacy, prostitution, dishonesty; they are religious, truly so, but I think their religion is selfish at bottom and amounts to an unusual mode of recreation.

Yet I continue and always shall continue to find pleasure everywhere. I find that Gwili certainly is second-rate; for he read me some stories of his, daily-journalistic in expression, mean in thought: – second rate *in English*, at least. I wish he were keener, more enthusiastic, more angular, more argumentative and vigorous. I sicken of his company if I ever liked it, and feel heartily glad of my escape from Friday's excursion. But this is bad tempered, and as a matter of fact I am bad tempered, – since this morning, when I wrote a resentful and bitter note to you, sweet heart; for indeed I had very little satisfaction from your hurried and scrappy letter, after such long expectation. I determined not to send that letter, but to wait and see how I was touched when I read it again; then I saw that you truly were affectionate and desirous of pleasing when it was written. I will wait now, until I write hoping to make you happy despite all.

Adieu, my own sweet little one, Helen.

ETC

---

1 'Gwili': the bardic name of Revd John Jenkins, a distinguished Welsh poet and Oxford theologian, an early and lifelong friend of ET.

3: *To Helen*

61 Shelgate Road

My dearest friend,

I don't leave here till tomorrow at 7 in the morning, but everything prevents me running over to see you – the bicycle is being used – I was exceedingly unwell yesterday and unable to go out – and besides (as perhaps for you more) I hate these hurried Crimes-like meetings in uncongenial surroundings almost more than short absence. Still I know my presence helps you, and would have come if possible. I shall not be away long; then I shall see you – perhaps at night – several times, while you are at Gipsy Hill.[1] Then we have not long to wait before we shall be relieved of the pains of doubt and the terrors of keeping a secret. For it is a pain and a terror. I have long been gloomy, though never despondent; and a protraction of this mood would have been fatal. But now we have an interesting and perhaps a pleasant future before us. If I stay at College, take my degree, and get work in Wales – it is excellent: if I am ousted from home, there will be a week or two of trouble, then the excitement of a rough beginning in literature, with you at my side – that also is well.

Within the next few months there will be tears shed, hearts broken (and mended again), and as much wicked ink spilled as it took to drown poor Clarence in a butt of Malmsey. I am a coward, and I know I shall often be near despair in this troublous time; but I think I shall recover and then there are few more mistakes left for me to make. And you, dearest – your innocence and motherly joy will surely keep you unbewailing in all your trouble: I hope so. My only wish is that the child may be comely to look upon; for to have an ugly child would be like gazing into a looking glass all day. We both of us have faults, and certain of our parents have greater faults; yet perhaps after all we shall be blessed. I have always worshipped beauty, and beauty has not always rewarded my worship; so perhaps now it will accord me a tardy and generous return for my attentions.

I suppose I need not remind you that the important date was April 6. What had been your thoughts that day? What had you seen? what heard? I was fresh from hearing music – not noble

7

music. Yet all music has advice for me. And the eternal stars and the black solemn scene of night were witness. – Remember to see as many fair sights and read as many fair books as possible. And above all, hear music: let it sink into your soul. May I be spared the stupid partiality of a father for his children, but oh! the pleasure of nourishing some rare spirit, – tender, or strong. Perhaps it is a pleasure greater than I deserve, yet my prayer must be expressed. I do not want a fortunate child, at least not a successful one: I do *not* want his life to be above all happy: but if it were myself, with genius and clearness added, I should be satisfied, grateful, ready to suffer anything, but not to die until I had seen his promise.

—Write to Swindon soon, and of course let me know when you leave St Peter's Square, which you had better do as soon as possible.

Adieu! Ever and wholly yours, Edwy. My anemone maiden, Goodbye.

I haven't time to look over this letter, so I want you to *send it back to me when read*: I will return it or not, just as you like, *but send it in any case.*

NLW

---

1 ET and Helen had been married on 20 June at Fulham Registry Office; Helen was expecting their first child.

4: *To Helen*

20 August 1899   *Gwynfryn, Amanford*

My dear Friend

It is impossible to tell you what my people say, but I can send this copy of the letter to Father I have just written, which will give you an idea of our correspondence. You can show it to Harry[1] if you wish. Read it before you go on with my short letter.

You had better go to Shelgate Road[2] as soon as possible: write and ask when you may come; I hope to be with you on Thursday. It is exceedingly distasteful to me, but if my Father will not consent to my leaving home to earn a living, why should he not be the victim of his own decision? According to Father, you have no *right* even to a farthing; but let that pass whether true or not, if ever; but we must tan our own skins, instead of letting others do it for us. Remember it is not a nice business at all; there is nothing heroic about it; we cannot expect the end of it to be anything but cheap and nasty patchwork. After writing to Father (or Mother) to say *when* you could come, viz. on Wednesday or Thursday, write to the woman at Carshalton; if you do so at once, compensation will probably be unnecessary.

What has Mrs Noble[3] to say about *me*?

Mary, I presume, did not know the whole truth, when she wrote you that charming letter, for which you must thank her very warmly from yourself and me; it must have been very welcome. Does Irene know the whole truth? Good God – to think that all the little journalists – Ethel Wheeler and the like – in London will be *able* to put me into a guinea prize story! The matter will soon reach Lincoln [College]. I am superior to them in one thing: I would not only *write* about a Borgia in gorgeous rhetoric, but I would be a Borgia, too, with a thousand mistresses (and not all women, either), I would poison and lie and scheme, and after all die at 40, if I had the power. Damn the respectable: I can't feel a bit reformed by this exposure. I vow I *will* enjoy that last year at Oxford! – For the present, however, I am having a rich holiday here, and storing up fine memories. Tomorrow I have another long drive to Talley Abbey and lakes, 20 miles off. If I stayed I should have many more; and the farmer I stayed with at Dryslwyn

one night last year is anxious I should go again; but I fear I can't.
Forgive these scraps. I am in a hurry and am not feeling bright.

Good bye sweetheart
I am and always yours Edwy,
My own sweet little one, Adieu.

Love to Janet and Harry; and renewed thanks.

NLW

1 Harry Hooton, a firm friend of ET from 1898. His wife Janet (née Aldis) was
   Helen's chief schoolfriend and witnessed the wedding.
2 61 Shelgate Road, the home of ET's parents, who had suggested that the
   couple live there until after ET's final Schools in June 1900.
3 Mrs Noble was not fully reconciled with her daughter for some years, but
   relations between Helen and her sisters, Irene and Mary, remained
   affectionate.

4A: *To Philip Thomas*

My dear Father,

In a former letter I ignored your remarks about my debt of honour to Lincoln: 1st because I thought it an unnecessary piece of hostility on your part, to suppose that I was blind to this debt; 2nd, because I thought it monstrous that (practically) the only reason you gave for my return to the College was this debt – not a small reason, I admit; but, as it seemed to me, outweighed by other considerations. I cannot think that is your only reason: if I did, my duty would lead me from home at once, always with a distant hope of repaying the £60 I have received from Lincoln.

Then as to selfdenial. What grounds have you for mentioning alcoholic drink, with the suggestion that there too I have gone to excess? I think you *know* nothing about that. Let me assure you that drinking is not a habit with me, and is unlikely to become one, if only because my purse is so small. As to 'libidinous French novels', I never read one because it was 'libidinous'! I have read some of the best French novels with a serious object, and one or *two* of Hugo's, Flaubert's, and Gautier's happened to be (what you call) libidinous in parts; but not more so than Shakespeare's plays, the Bible, the stage, Royal Academy Art, and after-dinner conversation etc etc; and in effects not more potent than good feeding, if I am rightly informed. Therefore I think there are no reasons for my giving up such books – except their expense. – Then as to tobacco: I am not now smoking to excess. It has indeed become a habit, but not so far as I am sure of, an injurious one. I find it very comforting, and if I took no tobacco just now, I should possibly take a good deal of something rather more alarming; I presume – since you say 'love is known by its fruits' – that you will not be angry that I prefer to ground my intended abstinences rather on reason than on a blind anxiety to please.

You ask – Is there some deception as to my earnings by writing? There has been no concealment. When I knew the *worst*, I naturally made every effort to meet it, and one or two publications of which I didn't tell you were the result. I know you will justly accuse me of apathy with regard to the expenses of keeping me at Oxford. All the same you know that one sudden

11

accidental evil stirs up a man more than a great longabiding one.

If Mrs Noble is right in saying that Helen has no money, and if you think it better that I should not go into Grub Street, the Carshalton plan falls to the ground. I will explain this to her, and though she is fearful of the trouble you will have when the child is born, she will probably see that it is all that is possible now: she will write and let you know when she will be ready to come, if it is convenient to you.

Ever your loving son

Edwy

NLW

5: *To Edward*

My dearest Friend,

This is the last time I shall write to you from this house where I have spent two such happy months.

And it shall be a happy letter, for though I am sorry indeed to leave the Hootons who have been so good to me, and such true friends, I cannot but look forward to being with you until you return to Oxford.

I am feeling ever so much happier about going to Shelgate Road. I received this letter from Mrs Thomas last night, which you will understand cheered me and made everything look much brighter. I send you the letter, which you can give me again when we meet.

This morning I received a short note from Mother, enclosing two bills of transfer relating to the shares in which my money is invested, requesting me to sign them, thereby closing the transaction. This Harry would not let me do, but took the papers away with him to ask at the office how it would be best to proceed. For you see the shares have been bought in my name, proving that as I said the money is mine, and that I can still sell out or not just as I like. Mothers says the *purchase* must be gone through with now; but Harry seems to think that as these papers are not signed, and as the purchase is not complete until they are, I can get it all without any difficulty. This will make Mother very angry, but I am afraid that can't be helped, for the money is absolutely necessary.

You will tell me I hope when you are to arrive in London, and where and when if at all I can meet you. Or would you rather I waited for you at Shelgate Road, or got there after you had seen your people.

I cannot write now, and you must pardon such a scrappy letter. We shall soon make up for this absence and everything. I think of nothing but your coming, our meeting, the days we shall spend together. Shall we have a room together? Surely we shall.

I have written to the Carshalton woman, proposing to pay her a week's rent and board which will be 18/-. I could not do less than this, for I feel that our sudden change of plans is rather hard on her. I hope she will be amiable.

My note from Mother contained nothing but a brief explanation of where etc. I was to sign my name. She has not all through this time said one really kind word to me; I don't know what she feels about either of us; I wish I did. Mary's home coming I hope will make things a little better.

And now for a little while goodbye. Farewell sweet heart mine. Ever and wholly I am yours, your own little one Helen.

Adieu dearest one.

NLW

6: *To Edward*

29 January 1900   61 Shelgate Road

My dearest friend,

All the while I was having tea – sitting close by the fire, Mater on one side of the table I on the other, such a happy little party – Philip who had just come in from a walk on the Common, under Sarah's guardianship, lay on my lap looking prettier than I have ever seen him, his eyes wide open, and his little mouth every now and then curving in the happiest of smiles.[1] I did so long for you to see him, though when you do come back to us, Philip will have begun to laugh and talk in his way, and will be even more lovely than he is now.

We both had a very good night, and I was astonished on waking to see from the windows a grey sky and a white Earth, for it had snowed heavily in the night. I have been up all today, walking about a little, and even going into Ernest's[2] room to enjoy the bright sunshine of the early afternoon, and to breathe a little sun warmed air. Now, as I sit writing the rain is beating loudly against the window and the wind comes in gusts down the chimney, blowing the fine ash all about the room. No one has been to see me; I can't imagine what has happened to my people; I think they must have sickness at the house. Irene has not come, though there is still hope for she generally comes late in the evening.

Dearest one I do so long for you; I find it harder than ever to be without you. You will say I have the little one to comfort me. Yes and he does comfort me, and give me endless joy and delight; but such joy is almost too great for me to have all to myself; I want you to share it; the boy reminds me all the time that you are not here. But this strange feeling of deepest joy and deepest longing, if indeed it is sad at all, I keep all in my own heart. I sing none the less happily to the little one, nor from my breast does he take anything but gladness.

I was very disappointed yesterday in trying on a new bodice, to find that my body had not nearly resumed its natural shape and size. I expect I am unreasonable to expect that it should so soon; but I am vain enough to hope it may become just as it was, though of course my breast will at any rate for the next nine months be fuller than formerly. Do you consider it mean to consider my appearance in this way? I do not think of it often, and I try to expel the thought or longing of all physical desire, though it is there being an insufferable part of my love for you; but there is the little one.

Mater says to me 'This little one will have to wait many years for a brother or sister' and intimated that she did not disapprove of my preventative measures. Nurse too who knows the circumstances in which we are said the same thing to me.

I wrote to Haynes today.[3] Did you remember when I met him he said he believed one could tell to a certain degree the character of the handwriting. I wonder what he will make of mine, whether or not the tale my eyebrows tell will be confirmed by my indecipherable writing: let us hope not.

How long my letter has become, and I did not intend to write today; but then, I must tell you of the little one; I must tell you always at once of my joy or my sorrow, because my heart is always with you, dearest Edwy.

I must say goodnight now. All is well with us, with you too I hope. Tell me soon. Kiss me and kiss Philip; I tell him of you and give him many kisses from you, and he sends many to you. Goodnight. Ever sweet heart mine. Adieu, adieu.

Irene is going into the country for Whitsuntide and wants Philip and me to go with her. To put up at a little inn and just ramble about among meadows and woods. I should love it, though I suppose I ought not to consider it, as my money is going fast. I keep an account of it, but it is horrible how it goes.

It is very late now. I stayed up to write.

Irene came to see me today, and Philip and I are to spend Sunday at Chancery Lane. Tomorrow we probably spend with Janet.

Write to me soon. I am feeling rather sad. You used sometimes to take my face between your hands and kiss my lips. I wish you could kiss me like that tonight. I wish I could make your difficulties less, or help you to bear them. It seems I cannot as you do not say what they are. You are not here to kiss me, so I must go to bed unkissed, and touch Philip with my lips for you.

Farewell sweet heart mine, Ever and wholly I am yours, your own little one Helen.

ETC

1 Philip Merfyn Ashcroft Thomas was born on 15 January 1900.
2 ET had five younger brothers: Ernest, Theodore, Reginald, Oscar and Julian.
3 E.S.P. Haynes, an Oxford and lifelong supportive friend of ET, especially at times of crisis. Became a fashionable society solicitor and wrote vivid memoirs of ET.

7: *To Edward*

My dearest Friend,

I have just sent the proofs off, having ordered 1 copy of 3 as you like it; 5 of 2, and 6 of 1, for the proof is not worth keeping as it fades.

When you hinted at other troubles besides the Schools, I do not think the holiday I have looked forward to for so long entered your mind. For that is easily got rid of, by simply remaining here. You could not be looking forward with so much pleasure to the relief of mind and body after Schools, as I am, or was, to a little time with you and Philip in the country, after my 18 months in London, and the various taxes on my strength. It has been a sort of heavenly landscape seen afar off through a dimly lit avenue of trees. You do not realise all the strain physical and mental that I have had during the last year. You leave me for a life perfectly congenial to one side of your nature, but for me there is no recompense, nothing to make up for you, nothing on which I can throw myself mentally and so forget my solitariness. That is only one, though the greatest, of those things which have made it so difficult for me to feel as well, and as cheerful as I used to feel. But if you say, you could not enjoy being with me as things are, or as we suppose they are, I certainly could not enjoy it either. My way is dependant on yours. As for money we could surely afford a little for such a holiday; there is no need to economise then, and the money would be well spent. And if things are with me badly, it is not only you, dear one, that will suffer; you will be troubled, so shall I, and in one sense more deeply than you, because I feel responsible, though unreasonably; also it is I will have the physical strain, and I think we must help each other to bear it as lightly as may be.

You see Edwy, your somewhat hard and cold way of saying things hurt me rather. I try my very best and succeed in writing ever to you as cheerful as may be, that I may not increase your despondency, but rather raise your spirits, but I am not utterly careless indeed.

I am glad about your work; it is good news. Mr Thomas says

he will be satisfied however you do in the Schools, being satisfied that you have worked well, he told me so.

The Logans are not at Oxford.[1] I don't know why it is so, except that Gwen has had mumps; neither is Miss Lucas I think. If she were I am sure she would make a point of meeting you. Her interest is in you for yourself; young married men in general do not interest her.

I have given Merfyn[2] a hundred kisses from you, and he has given me some from you to comfort me.

I saw Mary this morning, who lately has seen Miss Lucas, who told her that Haynes remarked to Miss Lucas 'Thomas won't let me go to his place, I can't imagine why; I think his people think I corrupt him.'

Did I tell you that the doctor thinks it very unlikely that anything has happened.

Philip and I are just going out. Goodbye. Don't think me too frivolous. Ever and wholly I am yours, your own little one Helen.

Farewell Edwy. Adieu.

ETC

1   Mrs Beatrice Logan, later Potbury, a close friend of Helen and Janet Aldis. Helen spent the early months of her pregnancy with her. Mr Potbury witnessed the Thomas marriage.
2   Helen preferred Philip as her son's name; ET's choice, Merfyn, was finally accepted.

8: *To Edward*

Dearest one

You have not told me yet when you return so I do not know if this letter is unnecessary or not. At any rate it is a pleasure for me to write, and I hope for you to receive.

The weather since you have been away has been dreadful; I mean it has rained every day and all day. Today it cleared up in the afternoon so Baby was able to be put out for an hour or so. We went to Shelgate Road to dinner and tea, and the servant took Baby out while the sun shone. The Baba is not very well. He looks as bonny as ever but his cold is in his chest, and he will eat nothing. He's been as jolly as ever today, and Mater thinks his slight indisposition is nothing more than the result of tooth coming. Your letter was good to have, though the news was disappointing. Here is a letter from Country Life which came by the last post on Saturday. I hope it contains some encouragement.

I am so glad you are enjoying yourself. Yes: I know Sandwich: the old gateway and the slow river, and the rather sleepy streets. And that long solitary road, with the sea on one side, and the marshes on the other. I used to walk to Sandwich and back often when I made long stays at Ramsgate, especially in a high wind, when it was a hard, but joyous struggle to keep erect with the wind full in my face, tearing my hair from its fastenings; but full of the sweetness of the sea, and of the joyousness of the crested waves one could see on the horizon marking the sands, where too at low tide generally a half sunk hulk is seen, giving to the waves that touch of cruelty which one forgets when they dance and laugh under a blue sky. O but I love the sea, and the high white cliffs, and the low marches where the sky larks build and where the hare bells grow.

Irene has just come for the night. So Adieu sweet heart mine. Come soon to me. Baby sends such kisses and love, and has such lots to tell you. He misses you I can see. Goodnight dearest one.

Ever and wholly I am yours Edwy, your own little one Helen.

NLW

9: *To Edward*

I cannot go to bed without saying 'Goodnight'. I have blown out the lamps, the fire is out, and the wind is screaming and hurtling against the house; the babes are asleep.[1] I cannot go to sleep without your kiss.

I have been sewing, and then reading for a little, the book of D'Annunzio's. Some of it I understand well, for whether a woman is fair, or has a radiant mind, or a lively soul, or has keen intellect, wit or passion, or whether she has none, yet this all women have in common, the power of loving, the same desires towards their beloved. So some of the book I understand well.

The children have been happy, and sleep very peacefully. I too shall sleep as a child, and wake glad and refreshed if you will kiss me, sweet heart.

Tuesday. The night has gone and come again, and with it peace and a bright moon, and clear frosty air. The fire which I have just lighted, feels it, and is roaring up the chimney in an ecstasy of flames; Rags feels it too but he is curled up among the cushions trying to forget it. Last night was long but quite happy. Bronwen was awake a great deal, but perfectly content. She lay by my side playing and laughing in spite of my sleepy indifference. She put her comforter on my head and laughed when it tumbled off, she stuck it in my eye and thought that a huge joke; she patted my face with her warm sweet hand, and pulled my hair, and kicked me just where ever her feet happened to have wandered. And all the time she was laughing and talking and shouting Daddy Daddy, and this is you please at about 2 o'clock in the morning; and but for little lapses in which she would sleep now and then her energy never wearied, and at 7 o'clock she was doing the same things again. The day, or rather the morning, was dull and close and rainy, but after dinner the sun came out and the air freshened, so I hope you had a good day on the pond.

Your letter sweet heart at noon was a joyous surprise. Thank you a thousand times. A letter from Mater came for me, and the *World* which I have read and will send on. Your Grandmother will be interested to hear that Lord and Lady so and so are having a shooting party and that the Countess of — is in delicate health. Did you see the *Chronicle* with your L. de T. review in it. It *is* good to have Nevinson's re-assurance about the D.C.[2] but still do not let that be enough; beard the Scot [Milne] in his den and make sure.

I hope these socks will be wearable. I took pains that they should and I think I have succeeded. Also I send a few old handkerchiefs.

The children have been very good and happy, though at breakfast Merfyn said: 'I am sorry Daddy has gone away.' When do you leave Swindon? I do hope you had a good day today. For you I was sorry when I saw the rain this morning, and glad when the sun shone this afternoon. Take care of yourself sweet heart.

The faggots have come, and the man has managed to put all but two in the passage, where they take up no more room than did the other 12. I gave him 6d. I don't know when I shall write again. I have said I will not write very often, but perhaps I shall, for it is good for me in the long evenings. Do not bother about letters, and yet leave me not too long; I am always anxious. The children send kisses, and I am ever and wholly yours, Edwy, my own beloved,

Helen

ETC

1 Rachel Mary Bronwen Thomas was born on 29 October 1902.
2 ET was now principal literary reviewer for the *Daily Chronicle*, of which James Milne was editor-in-chief.

10: *To Edward*

10 December 1903 *The Green (Bearsted)*

Dearest one,

The rain has come down with such determination and the darkness is so fiercesome that instead of dining with Miss Broughton, I am writing to you which is no great hardship. In fact the last time I looked out I was rather relieved to find it was better than before, for I have got to love and look forward to my long silent evenings when I feel that no amount of space between us could separate us entirely. And I love my letter writing poor as I know it is really. I love people and could not live alone even, so that if I am not writing and so bringing you and the other people near to me, I am reading of people in novels or in less trifling form. And if I sew it is of people I think all the time; though I cannot call it thought exactly, it is something far more primitive. I remember things that have passed and smile over them and live them over again happily to myself, or I picture you for instance in your sitting room with Morgan: I make the pose of your head as it pleases me best; I know just how you will be sitting if you are talking, and it is talking I generally imagine you. I hear the pleasant tone of your voice, for it is a sweet-sounding voice to hear. I look up from my work and notice your profile, and your rumpled hair; I love to hear you laugh, and oh sweetheart it is hard not to be able to break through and tell you how I love you, as if I had never told you before. Or else it is the pride of a mother I feel in you, a longing in all to see you and show my pride in you, as if I thought 'he is part of me, he lay in my womb and sucked my breasts.' That is how I often feel about you sweetheart, and that is because I am a mother before all things, and it is as your mother sometimes I would caress you. And so I sit sewing, looking, and smiling and longing, and listening, and we are very close then sweetheart. And then dreams come and dreams are sweet too, but I like best the dreams I make for myself, for I make only fair ones, and sometimes the sleep dreams are sad, and sometimes ugly, and only sometimes did I wake unwillingly all worn and trembling with a strange emotion. Sweetheart do you know I cannot conceive of my world without you. I don't remember what life was like before you came and said live and I lived. You took me out of my narrow little lane, and brought me into a great wide space all bright with things I have never seen or felt before, all pouring upon my senses.

The wind has gone and the rain and there is no sound in the ivy leaves. The stars out. I am glad it is too late to go now. I like sitting here by the fire murmuring to you. I have put the willow china on the mantlepiece, it looks good there I think. Miss Harris did not come today, and asked if she might come tomorrow. I hope she will be nice; I like her though I am a wee bit afraid of her because she is pretty and so confident. Tell me soon when you will be home. I think it would be good to be together at Christmas. It would be good to be together more, dear. I was foolish to say anything about any secret I was cherishing for you. Please forget it; it is so trifling really that having mentioned it to you I feel almost ashamed of it.

Mater will be here tomorrow and if your ears are burning it is because they are wanting to listen to less noisy voices than Morgans. How the time slips away. Have you been happy dear one. I have been happy in my dreaming. All is well with us tonight, is it not fact; my mind can grasp nothing or count on nothing but your return.

So forgive this, sweetheart. Merfyn has just said 'I wish Daddy was here to come, and Christmas too.'

Mater sends her love, and Merfyn and Bronwen kisses and sweet messages, and I am ever and wholly yours

Helen

NLW

11: *To Helen*

16 December 1903   *C/o Mrs Labrum, Warminster*

My dearest friend.

This must be a short note of business. First of all I enclose 3 cheques

30.0.0	from	Black
2.15	"	World
1.1.0	"	D.C.
33.16.0		

Please bank £33 and take out 16/- which ought to enable you to pay Daisy: if not take out another 10/-. Bank it at once, i.e. on Thursday, because I am sending out cheques at once to Haynes, Ambrose Parsons and others which will swallow up the greater part.

Secondly, I have to dress for Nevinson's dinner.[1] So please send at once if possible in a flat cardboard box, the following things –

dress suit – coat waistcoat trousers / slippers / black or blue socks / one or two white ties.

N.B. the dress suit is in the little attic; the ties are in the cardboard box in my chest of drawers; the socks are somewhere near. You have probably seen the slippers about. Please send them to Irenes, of course

c/o H.V. McArthur / 64 Chancery Lane[2]

It is a nuisance but I am now bound to go.

Please don't spend 5/- on Merfyn, at least before I come back.

I shall try to return on Sunday, but Morgan[3] and I may with Haynes buy a cheap Sunday ticket to Oxford – let us hope not. Remember I shall be at 13 Rusham Road on Friday night and at Irene's on Saturday night.

I am now busy with accounts and posting cheques.

Goodbye, sweet heart. Kiss Merfyn and Bronwen again. I am ever and wholly yours Edwy

The literary editor of the 'Chronicle', I am very sorry to say, is an ignorant Scotchman James Milne, who writes 'Writers and

Readers' in D.C. – Nevinson, who worked in the same room with him, once described him as knowing 'more about the outside and less about the inside of books' than any other man.

NLW

1   Henry Wood Nevinson, who first employed ET on the *Daily Chronicle*, was about to leave the paper.
2   Hugh McArthur, Irene Noble's husband; they often offered ET generous hospitality.
3   Professor J. Hartman Morgan, Welsh friend of ET at Oxford and during his early years as a reviewer. Influential proposer of Civil List pension for ET and, later, for Helen.

12: *To Edward*

Dearest

For Merfyn this day has been more than all his birthday; for me it has been a letter day, and whenever I have had a moment of quiet solitude I have read your dear letter again, and loved it more each time.

The praise of Hind to Milne was indeed good. How surprised Hind will be to hear who he was praising, for he was no lover of your work, was he, when at the *Academy* office? Give Dal[1] my invited comrade 'love' and thank him for that touching little Table Mountain episode, which I appreciated none the less, knowing it is pure fiction. I am glad you like the 'Yorick', and altogether your affairs seem to be more hopeful, and you ought to feel encouraged, sweet heart. I expect though Irene has not read *Oxford*[2] she was pleased with your gift, wasn't she? Still, she might have the decency to read it, though I suppose she has not much spare time. Moreover there is lots in it she would like, though as yet she has never confessed to an appreciation of your work.

It is nine o'clock and you are dining with Haynes. Oh no, you did that last night I see. I wonder if you enjoyed playing host again, and if Haynes was appreciative. He always has been pleased with his entertainment here, and I expect that he tasted your wine and pronounced it good after much mumbling and holding to the light.

Merfyn has had a very happy and boisterous day. Chocolates have poured in from every quarter. A large box came by post with a city grocer's label, addressed I think by Hugh [McArthur]. So I will write tomorrow thanking them. All except that box I have kept in reserve, and even with the one box he has been most moderate. Mater sent him a top, and another book in the same series as the Squirrel book, which he liked very much. Mrs Adams called, and hearing it was Merfyn's birthday sent in a toy and book. So he is a very rich boy. He has been very good, and the party was a great success, and he went to bed tired and happy. He was glad to have your kiss this morning, and altogether he finds four a very pleasant age to be.

The day has been splendid too. Not so much wind, and such lovely sunshine, and nice clean, cold air. So the children have been out a good deal, and Bronwen went to sleep in Merfyn's cot without a murmur. She is so sweet, and says 'cup' quite plainly, and makes a very good attempt at 'biscuit'. She enjoyed the party too, and was as excited and happy as Merfyn. Mrs Ivens called this evening and told me that she had seen in the *Express* that the *Chronicle* was going to become a $1/2$d paper. Is that true, I hope not. Her coming and Mrs Adam's call quite hindered my shirt making, and with the second, I have not got beyond the cutting out. But I hope to do a lot tomorrow. I won't forget the Virgil with the boots etc (which as yet are not done).

And now I must say 'goodnight'. When you say goodnight to me I shall be asleep, but it will slip into my dreams, or come as a sweet dream into my deep sleep. And who shall say that my soul shall not answer yours, but now as I say goodnight you are in a crowd, with sounds filling your ears, and sights filling your eyes. But perchance you are as one in a dream and hear me, or feel my kiss. All is well even though the world is between us for an hour. All is well ever even with us. Goodnight my own dear love.

16th. I saw your Oxfordshire review this morning and I want to read the book now, but what with spending such a lot of time out of doors with the children and sewing hard when they are in bed, I have not even finished an exciting chapter of 'Some Dons'. Today I was out practically the whole morning racing up and down the hard frozen roads, pulling the small cart while Merfyn pushed behind. Bronwen encouraged our speed with shouts and laughter, and we arrived home glowing and out of breath and so hungry. This afternoon I took Mrs Ivens the round up to Haking Road and back down the Thurnham Hill. We walked quickly, for I had sent the children out with Daisy. You can imagine that our conversation was not intellectual exactly, but walking in this cold crisp air was glorious; and Oh! I wish you had been with me! Sweetheart I felt that if I ran and ran over the hills, surely I should come to you waiting for me, with arms outspread for me to run into as children do. You seemed so near, and at each turn of the road my heart leaped and I dare hardly look with thinking you might be there, and not knowing how I could bear such sudden joy. And when I got home and no curve of the way had revealed you to me I was not disappointed. In fact I knew you have been very near, my heart beat with joy that only you can give me; my body trembled with the delight of your touch; perhaps you had smoothed my blown hair from my eyes as you have done sweetheart, do you remember; perhaps you had lifted me up and run as if I really was the child I felt; perhaps you had just touched my hand that I might know our souls were in perfect harmony. I know not how, in what sweet tender way you had given pleasure to my whole being; bubbling, uplifting, dancing happiness, and pleasure making me tremble. And the children came in all noisy and laughing, our own children, dearest one, the fruit of such love as made this afternoon possible to us! And then our tea was all children's talk, and at last a song, for they were tired, and now they are asleep, dreaming their own sweet pleasures over again.

Then all this evening I have sewn your shirt, and have done a lot to it, though as I have not enough stuff to finish it, I will not include it in the Monday's parcel. I have asked Mater if she has a little bit, for she told me not so long ago that she had some pieces. Then the finishing will not take me half an hour and you can have it soon.

And now the night is near again. This morning Merfyn before I got up gave me two kisses to give to you. So now they are joined, one for your mouth and one for your forehead.

Goodnight sweet heart, dearest one goodnight.

ETC

---

1 Charles Dalmon, a poet friend of ET, who had frequented Beatrice Logan's house in Hammersmith.
2 *Oxford* in Black's Colour Book series, painted by John Fulleylove, RI, described by ET, published in 1903.

13: *To Edward*

Dearest one

Here you are writing dear sad letters to me, I trying to cheer you up, which I am sure is not as it ought to be, and we must be conventional at all costs, I always say so!

But today, sweetheart, though in the very very inside of me I feel happy as I always did, now outside cheerfulness is getting rather hard to maintain.

My throat is behaving like the very — and now my ear on that side and all my neck and head are in pain. I had very little sleep last night, and so stayed in bed till after the church bells had stopped. I suppose I am in for it all now, but the doctor does not come until tomorrow so I can't say for certain.

I give you these 'arrowing details, dear, so that you may know all there is for you if you can come home. I want you even so – of course I do, and even if my throat goes the whole hog, I'll promise not to entertain you like this every day with details. I think I should be as happy as a lark, or rather an inarticulate one; and as for eating, I wish I could combine the lark and the camelion. Whatever you decide to do dearest one, I shall know it is best and be content.

Last night when I heard the 8 train coming in, my heart anticipating my thoughts in the cheekiest way, began thumping…, and then, as someone stopped outside the gate, it got mixed up in my throat and I held my breath: but the someone having played his trick on me went on, and I, I did not cry as you might expect, but I just snoodled down quite content that it will not be long before you come.

This morning I got £10 from Mac[1] with an English stamp and the post mark Canterbury. Queer isn't it! Just G.I.M. in the corner. And that you must know is to be spent in secret according to a private and previous arrangement. And if £10 doesn't cheer you, you say, nothing will. But Mrs Farewell has been moralizing about the relative value of money and health, so my poor little windfall is quite an annoyance now. But just think of all the charming little contrivances I can buy to make 'the home' comfortable. Contemplate in your mind the rows of little pots of ferns I can put on your right and left hand to refresh your eyes while we eat a beefsteak. And oh and its oh I want my dear old boy.

I shall like to learn of your walk with Haynes, who answered my first letter which was all about himself, but my second all about myself he ignores. Daisy has gone home to her hairdressing morning but Mrs Farewell manages very well, and I don't at all see, especially with my inspiring presence, why you could not do your work. We shall be like Darby and Joan, and pretend that Merfyn is at Balliol, the bright and shining star of the college and University and that Bronwen is married – and to who she shall be married, we can arrange that when you come back.

I am sure I know just how you feel in those cramped little rooms. I should spend most of my time wondering how I should get out again. As I said before I am as cheerful as you like, but my throat is going at hammer and tongs, and I won't write any more for fear you should forget how happy I really am. 'So kiss me quick and go me honey'. Only don't go but come soon. Farewell till you come to me, farewell always sweetheart mine. I am ever and wholly yours,

Helen

P.T.O.
Late in the day. I feel so ill my dearest, I think I cannot bear being without you any longer. If you come tell Mater first, she will wonder.

ETC

1 Sir Ian MacAlister, who was at St Paul's and Oxford with ET, with Haynes and Hooton a most supportive friend at critical times. Eventually Secretary of the RIBA and knighted, at this time he was in Canada.

14: *To Helen*

Well Knowe, Cartmel

Dearest one

I have just been asleep for an hour (it is 4) because I did the same yesterday and then had the clearest and happiest hour I have had since I came, as I was walking back from the post across 'The Park'. Yet your letters were enough (one letter and a parcel containing another arrived together at 9.30), and I was more sweetly dissatisfied than usual; only I was still tired and thought I would call sleep to the aid of your letters – sweet one, dearer letters they seem than you ever have sent and I have no language but my body to thank you with and that is glowing with thanks even yet. If I could only love *you* and show my love as much as you deserve how happy would you (and I) be! But with all my silly head and trembling body and rotten soul I do love you, and Merfyn and Bronwen will love you as you should be loved. How gay your letter is with your happiness and theirs. As I write this, I feel keenly how stupid it is not to be off to you at once. Yet I am getting more out of my visit than I thought I should. I can't and don't walk at all except to the post, but my talks (though far too 'littry' and all that) are getting easier and deeper and more satisfying, and a few expressions of violent dislike of men and books have cleared my mind a good deal. I now find I can say to Gordon[1] what I cannot say to most people with the exception of some bad language. Mr Bottomley came back last night and we have had some three-sided talks. – I admire and could like him but he emphasises too much his 'literary' tastes and dislike of 'commercialism' and though they are part of a real refinement, in themselves they are a little laughable. He and everyone speaks so lovingly (and more than that) of you.

I have spent 1d. since I came here, and got three clay pipes for it.

Goodbye dear old sweet and beautiful one. Keep yourself as neat as you have made the house and I won't grumble ever again; and don't wear your glasses. Kiss Merfyn and Bronwen for me many times and get them to kiss you back for me.

I am ever and wholly yours, my own sweet little one / Edwy

[1] Gordon Bottomley, poet, one of ET's close friends.

15: *To Helen*

Dearest one,

I have just been keeping up New Year's eve with Aldises and Webbs,[1] playing whist with Mr Webb, listening to Maud playing her viola, and finally – think of it – dancing a corkscrew, treading on everyone's toes, turning the wrong way, defacing virtue and beauty on every hand. But I had done a good day's work first, re-reading hastily 2 books of Jefferies and getting on with my index of subjects and arrangement of biographical matter. In the morning I walked into Dunwich to post my letter to you, though it did not go until 7.45 p.m., and back along the beach, collecting three logs on the way. This picking up of logs on the beach becomes a mania. Mr Aldis spends all his time at it, and goes about with a bright steadfast eye fixed on logs in mid air, in the sky and on the ground. But I prevent my stiff neck (partly a strain I think) from getting quite well, by carrying heavy logs up to the house. Janet goes tomorrow and then I must try to work faster. Janet is very nice and friendly but isn't it like her to say, as Maud began to play and the room was full of the family, visitors and servants, 'Maud's £100 viola'? Not boastfully, but just quiet joy at the high price. Oh today I helped to get one of the Webb's cows out of a ditch where she was likely to be drowned, and then Phyllis, Hope and Alice came and thanked me – all in a row in their hockey jerseys, shy and beaming – and asked when you were coming and asked me to send love to you, and Paul said he had a letter you wrote him and Alice remembered you well. They were all away playing in a hockey match all day and came back singing wildly about their success – a team of Aldises and Webbs (including Mrs Webb, who is very energetic.)

What splendid gardening weather! I ought to be digging instead of collecting firewood.

Goodnight, sweetheart. It is nearly 1 now.

1.1.08. I have left it till 11 p.m. to write and I am almost asleep. I have been indoors since 11 except for a short time sawing up logs. I have got through half a dozen of Jefferies' books now and may be able to begin writing next week. Where time is coming from to do my reviewing I don't see. But there is not much to do just yet. I had my dinner with the Aldises today, Mr. and Mrs., Maud, Ethel, Norah, and Joy, and two visitors. Cyril left with Janet. I get on well enough but not well. There is plenty to eat. I got my own tea and supper in no time – for supper I had some broth I warmed up, and then cheese and apple dumpling made yesterday. I again walked to Dunwich after breakfast and back along the beach, on my way seeing a squirrel that sat and looked at me close by like this;

Merfyn and Bronwen would have laughed to see his paws crossed over his white breast and his red tail hanging down below the branch. The sun shone bright as I walked along the beach and I was warm enough. My stiff neck is nearly gone and I have only had one twinge of toothache and that was after standing out in the cold getting in some wood. It was good of Merfyn to write. I wish he could be down here, and Bronwen, too, to play with the little Webbs (who call you Auntie Helen). They would like the wide moor and the windmills in the flat meadows by the sea below us to the south, and the herd of black cows there; and the huge white waves, and all the pretty pebbles on the beach, and the bits of wreck washed up and old beer bottles and corks, oranges, baskets, the tops of barrels, huge beams, and seaweed. The wind and the sea never cease to sound.

Janet's lamp is a silly one. The light bobs all the time and tires my eyes, so I have written to the Stores for one of those reading candlesticks.

I wrote to Mother this morning.

34

Well I must try to get up at 7.30 tomorrow so as to be about when Hope[2] brings the milk. So goodnight to you all. Are you all well, not even a cold? Does the eiderdown do?

Thursday
Some of them have just been to Southwold and called for letters on the way back and among them yours. I was glad to get it especially as you missed Wednesday and I didn't know how often you meant to write. You all sound well and cheerful in spite of the weather. So am I, for today I am a good deal better. I haven't been out enough, but I am now trying to get through the preliminaries as fast as possible so as to be able to start the writing. I only went down to the beach after lighting my fire this morning and then along it again for a mile or so after dinner. Washing up etc. takes me a little time. It was after 10 before I got to work though I was up at 7.45. There is very little to tell you about my dealings with my neighbours. I haven't talked much with any of them and hardly at all with the Webbs. Mr Aldis I don't get on with very well. I evidently annoy him, partly by refusing to eat anything with sugar in it which of course looks ostentatious. Little does he know how absolutely careless in food I have always been. I told you all I could remember about my visit to the doctor. I described my habits during the past 7 or 8 years pretty completely, and my state of mind, depression etc., and he asked me if I slept well and if I had pains after food and so on. Of course I was particularly rotten when he saw me – with cold, waiting, the hurry and annoyance of the morning, toothache etc. He didn't say a word as to what might be wrong, but I suspect it is my kidneys. It is quite possible I have eaten too much marmalade, honey, jam, treacle etc. and the medicine he gave me makes such things unnecessary.

With the Aldises I sit silent and glum mostly unless I am spoken to. Mrs Aldis pays most attention to me. I am not attracted to any except Maud who is very nice and handsome except when she speaks. Tonight I am going to play whist with Mr Webb a little while. They all talk of you affectionately.

I read Mrs Bone's book in the train. The review is not very bad. Chesson is one of the best D.C. men, but irritating. The pictures are admirable and a lot of the book is, but it is not masterly, always clever and serious, often (in the descriptions for example) beautiful.

Alice has just brought me the milk. So I must get supper. The wind was so strong she could not pull the door open. Goodbye.

Friday Please find my square-toed shoes – the very broad ones with very square toes and smallish nails and rather bad soles – and send them to David Uzzell / 6 John Street Terrace / New Swindon / Wiltshire.[3]

Merfyn's report is not satisfactory.[4] Mr. Scott's comment is only politeness and it was probably he who crossed out the remark that Merfyn seemed run down at the beginning of the term. Nearly all the comments point to listlessness and incapacity. What they mean or may become I don't know, but they are very much like me now. But of course it may pass off or it may develop in an interesting if not a pleasant way. We must try to let him get strong and to not repress him and do things for him as little as possible.

It's fearfully cold but I make an enormous fire in this room and keep warm by sitting close to it. Will you send me my smaller drawing board with a letter? It won't weigh much and it will enable me to write on my knee close up to the fire if necessary.

It was horrid playing whist. I could not keep on thinking about the cards especially as I felt uncomfortable with Mr Aldis, so I revoked among other things. However I did not stay long and I got back and read till midnight. I feel well and not really lonely at all – though my neighbours don't affect my solitude. Lancelot Aldis comes today.

Now I must get my lunch (dinner this evening today) and post this in Dunwich this afternoon. I am ever and wholly yours my own sweet little one. Give my kisses to the children.

Thursday / 20 ii 08   *The Bungalow / Walpole*
Dearest one, I walked over here this morning, ten miles, before dinner. The first half was along level roads with fresh ploughed

fields or stubble on either side and practically no wood and of course no hill in sight! The larks and missel thrushes and first chaffinches sang. It was a gusty cloudy day after a beautiful still early morning and I got tired by the first five miles. Then the country began to heave a bit and there was a big sloping field with ancient grooves in it – where a castle had been – and a moat and a fine thatched church with its round brick tower separate from it.

That was better. I was not so tired when I got here. We had dinner at 1.30, the children all running off immediately after hurried eating to play hockey. I stayed behind and looked through Mr Webb's books and read a little and then helped to get tea: there is no servant here. Then after tea I played Matthew the Miller with them till all departed except Phillis who is now practising.

Those 'private' letters are only announcements of a meeting for discussing a proposed society of Dramatic Authors and then postponing it: I don't know what is so 'private'?

How much luggage will you have on Friday? For the Webbs are here with the trap every Friday and can drive you. But of course if you have more than a very little I can order a trap.

Phillis is such a child, as naïve as Bronwen almost and bubbling over with interest in very small things. I happened to mention the fire at Nightingale Parade and she was such a listener to my not vivid account. They all wish you could bring Bronwen, but of course it is impossible. Merfyn will return to school on the Monday I suppose.

By the way Hope was interested in a poem of Blake's and I proposed to send her a selection (cost 2/6), but she says it is too extravagant – 'ask Auntie Helen'; so you must send me written permission to make this present! Please do: on a separate sheet of paper.

Friday

I am back again and have had your beautiful letter written under the influence of Hall's Distemper Wine, but as I have walked 12 miles and have just shoved two barrowloads of sand up from the beach I have a disadvantage. Moreover it is time to go to the post, so I cannot be as lyrical as you are but can only say I think every hour of your coming here and am sure you will be happy and so shall I. There is no news but another long letter from the Oxford man, mentioning that Fyfe had heard about his paper on me and had written to him for leave to see the paper (which is to be forwarded to me). I ought by the way to leave here on Monday the 2nd. so as to see Jesse[5] whom I cannot otherwise see for I don't know how long. Would you travel with me or stay the night here? I must go now with one ship and many birds for Bronwen and all. I am ever and wholly your

    Edwy

The bay is now full of these ships

NLW

1 ET was staying in a cottage near the Aldis family in Minsmere near Dunwich, Suffolk. The Webbs had given HT her first job, as a nursemaid at their home in Margate, in 1896. For the background to this letter, see *Edward Thomas: A Portrait*, pp. 144 ff.

2 Hope Webb, the seventeen-year-old schoolgirl of the Webb family to whom ET was strongly attracted; she had been Helen's favourite in 1896. When she returned to school, her father insisted that ET discontinue writing to her. There is no suggestion of an improper relationship. As ET wrote to Harry Hooton in March 1908, 'I know I was foolish, but the punishment as it always is is excessive.' She never married, and is not mentioned in the correspondence I have seen between HT and Janet Hooton.

3 Often referred to as 'Dad', Uzzell – countryman, gamekeeper and poacher – was a friend and early mentor of ET in country matters, during his adolescent visits to his paternal grandmother in Swindon.

4 He was at Bedales, and the family was living in Berryford Cottage, Ashford.

5 Jesse Berridge, poet, bank clerk and then clergyman; annual walking companion and lifelong friend of ET and HT.

16: *To Edward*

Monday 6 January 1908   *Berryfield Cottage*

Dearest one,

You gave me such a lovely surprise this morning that I've been smiling to myself all day because of it. Merfyn called to me, 'There's a letter from Daddy, I know his writing, and he always puts Mrs H B Thomas' – I said 'I know you, you're just playing a trick on me to hurry me down'. 'Truly there is a letter from Daddy it's just like his writing', but I thought it was a trick. All the same I hurried with my hair, and down with myself and there it was a letter on Monday when I thought I must wait till Wednesday. I do thank you sweetheart. We read it together, and Bronwen loved the little robin all by himself on the beach; and Merfyn laughed because you got lots of porridge for breakfast. We always find laughter in your letters dear; some good joke that makes us merry all day; they are splendid your letters, the way they cheer us up and keep us happy.

We saw last night the most beautiful new moon that ever was, with one little bright star; the same little star that looks in at us at tea every evening before the other stars are out. We wondered if you saw the new moon. Yesterday *was* cold, but still and misty. We put food out for the birds, and a coconut for the tits; and what do you think a green woodpecker flew right past the window and then on to the trunk of the plum tree at the bottom of the garden, wishing I am sure that he had the boldness of the blackbirds who were shoving all the little birds from the plate of food. We planned to go today to Petersfield, and after lunch there to go and see the skaters on the heath pond. But when we woke up, after going to bed with ice on the windows, all was bathed in damp heat, and all was dripping and misty, and a fine rain came down all the time. I had to go into Petersfield to change the cheque, for which thanks, for Maud wanted her money, but I went very quickly on my bicycle, and there posted the shoes to the old man, and sent off your board too.

Just now the children are very interested in Jesus, and I was telling them at tea how kind he was, and good to the poor. 'Oh that's just like Dicky's grandfather was, he *was* kind, he gave

£100 to a tramp lady at the door; and at first she thought he was only going to give her a penny, and she looked a little bit sad, but when she saw a hundred pounds, oh she was so excited; it would not all go into her purse so she had to put into her pocket.' And tonight their game was Bronwen's invention. Merfyn was a poor boy in bed, and Bronwen was Jesus bringing him nice things. I read to Merfyn some of the little tales of saints out of Lady Gregory's book. Best of all he liked the tale of the little boy who fell into the well, and was held up under the chin, by a little grey man who was Saint Colum. Then he liked the one like 'Come all you little blacky tops'. Last night their game was being 'knights'. Bronwen and Molly and each fighting a chair, or else each other. Merfyn said he was a Welsh knight. Bronwen was Scotch. I had been reading out of the *Wonder Book* about the young knight who was the son of Gawain though none knew it, and who was called 'Le Beau Discoun'.

I get tired of the children's company sometimes and wish I could be alone or with people; but I get a lot of real joy from them. This afternoon I took them a walk all in the fine rain and gusty wind, but Merfyn was in a languid mood and wanted to be home. He is to have a little party on his birthday: Gracie and Roy Anthony and Vasco I expect.

I had a little note from Mater today: just a greeting out of her kind heart, fearing I was lonely.

Well! Phyllis has sealed her fate. Her 'career' then is given up. I had hoped it would not be after all, as they were to wait so long, and Phyllis might find one more to her liking.

I was interested to hear what the Webbs were like. Hope was my favourite. I remember that Phyllis and Alice were *very* fair; but that Hope had large dark eyes and long dark eyelashes, and was wicked, not a bit over kind – rather the black sheep, who overruled the others, and got scolded for it. Paul had reddish hair and eyelashes with dark shy eyes; not a pleasant face altogether, he told lies, and howled when he did not have his 'goodnight' chocolate in consequence. Yet I was fond of them all.

Here are a few things from the wash. There is still a pair of stockings and a flannel shirt and pyjama trousers.

I used to go and sit up in that lighthouse at Southwold, not at

40

night though, for no one was allowed there when the lantern was lighted; but in the daytime when the fine old lighthouse man was polishing the reflectors and trimming the lamp. Your work seems going well. I'm so glad about it. Let me do any copying out for you, please. I keep a diary now, just facts of what I do day by day; really just for something to do in the evening. I keep accounts too. I sew of course in the evenings, but they are long. I learnt a pretty new song out of the Country Song Book, called 'Twenty, Eighteen', and am getting myself word perfect in Green Grow the Rushes Oh, for the children are so fond of it.

I've got some ointment from Dr Pankridge for my scarred hand and my elbows, so when you come back it seems to me, what with accounts, etc., you'll have a wife as fair outside as she's good inside. But when will that be says the love heart in me? It seems ages and ages since you left. But time will settle itself down reasonably after a while I expect. Besides I've got heaps to do before you return, so don't you dare to return before I say you may; and I'm not at all sure that I can do it all in two months, more like three or even four, so just make up your mind to it.

Mrs Read comes tomorrow to wash, for the last time she thinks before she 'goes upstairs' as she says. It's wonderful how she works, and I told her not to come again, but she says she must work, she's miserable idle.

Well, now I'll pack your parcel and put this inside. Here are your poets, some of them anyway. Here also is Bronwen's mask for you. She hopes to write some day. Merfyn and Bronwen send kisses to you; the wind will take them tonight: such a fine roaring warm west wind.

Goodnight sweetheart. Your letter was good to have. Keep well and happy all the time. Ever and wholly I am yours. Helen

Air these things very well. The Lahman cotton attracts any damp there is about.

I'm being very good about using cinders etc.

Tuesday A book sent direct from the publisher by Shiel called 'The White Wedding' has come, showing that Shiel is still friendly. I'll not send it as it costs 4d. and you won't want it I expect.

41

I've written a stiff note to Pocock about the roof.

The Doughty has just come too. I opened it for the sake of lightness.

Bronwen is wonderfully well, as lively as ever and full of mischief and laughter, and so good too; indeed they are both that, and though Merfyn is the 'goodest' his faults annoy one far more than Bronwen's do. He very much wants a letter from you, so be sure to write to him on Wednesday.

Mrs Read did not come this week after all. She is not in bed yet, but I should be surprised if she comes again before the baby arrives. If she does not, I'll wash your stockings etc. and send them on. Now I'd better do some mending. I've been doing it all day, except when I took the children out this afternoon. Goodnight sweetheart. The children send loves and kisses, and so do I and am ever and wholly yours

Helen

Pocock has not come, nor answered my note. There's a parcel at Petersfield. I'll send it off tomorrow (Thursday).

ETC

17: *To Edward*

Dearest one

Merfyn's birthday has been a very happy day for us all, and he enjoyed it from beginning to end. He will write to you himself tomorrow, he says to thank you for the book. He likes it as I knew he would, and already has got me to read it nearly all to him. Bronwen and he laugh very much at the doings of the wise men, and Maud lingers near while I read to join in the laugh at the end of the story. He liked your letter too, and wishes you had been here to join in the games and share in the cake and crackers and everything that goes to make a birthday such a joyful festival. There were nine children to tea, and as it was fine we were able to use the spare room for games – Maud and I have cleared it out and packed everything up to make room. It has been a warm damp, misty day, so we have not been out, though while I was busy with the cakes this morning, the children played in the shed. I've been tired and headachy all day, but was of course able to join in the games which began at 3, and went on till 6.15. So now I am very tired, but glad that it was so happy for the children.

Your letters amaze me, as much as they delight. A miracle is being worked, and what I have longed and tried for so long has come at last and you are happy, and content and well. I can't quite grasp it, though I am just full of rejoicing over it. yes I *am* full of rejoicing, but there's a little sneaking part of me that wishes – especially on lonely evenings like this when I'm too tired to do anything, and ought not to be writing to you, only that I can't endure this dead weight of silence and tiredness – that – but I don't know what that part of me wishes, and anyway it doesn't matter.

I wish I could put myself out of my thoughts altogether, and just be perfectly, serenely content and thankful, and never anything else. I wish I could feel that it satisfies me utterly to know of your well being, and of how your work goes and your health, and your free time all so splendidly, just as I have wanted it to go. But it doesn't; I thought my love was the kind that could be, but I find that I'm asking for something else; some suggestion for instance that it will be wholly sweet to you to be here again; or that after your day of work it would be good to have me with you. I long to have you, but after the keen sea air, after the perfect control of your day, your quiet, your work, your society all yours to dispose of just as suits you best, how will this seem to you. I want to see you so well, so content, so happy; I want to join in it with you, but can I, shall I ever, or will it be different when you come back, without all that has done this for you.

But it will only be for a day, then you will go again, and get more and more of that which will make life so full of all that I have longed for you to have, and it will last for ever, won't it, and I shall become a part of it and the children and everything.

Oh I do a nice thing surely, to try to make it less happy for you, to write down for you the thoughts that come because I'm too tired to think better ones, as I usually do. For all day – and it is true sweetheart – my heart is beating loudly as if you were near, and it's all because I'm happy and thankful. And I look at the clock a dozen times a day, and say now he does so and so, now this, now that, getting comfort by pretending to know and see and feel how it is with you. It's only now when I'm alone and idle and stupid that I'm otherwise. For after all it's my love for you that is the reason why I live at all, and if it is so great a thing, it cannot be what I say it is now, can it dear? wanting to spoil all with its selfishness. You do believe that I'm good really; I wish I could be good even when I'm tired. I kiss you goodnight and ever and wholly yours

Helen

ETC

18: *To Edward*

Monday night, 20 January 1908   *Ashford*

Dearest one

I don't know how I came to neglect sending the enclosed on to you. It came with *A Year's Exile* a novel by George Bourne. I did not send the book on knowing you would not want it, and forgot to mention it. I'm very sorry. Your jolly letter yesterday was the pleasant beginning of a pleasant day. It was very misty, so misty that the moisture dripped from everywhere and our hair was beaded with it, and Rags soaked with it, but for all that Irene and I had a splendid walk of 15 miles or so. We went along the Liphook road to the Jolly Drover, then we turned to the right along a beautiful wooded road, and then to the left down into a wooded hollow, when in the mist all the colours of the lichen on the beech trees, and the green moss at their roots, and the brown bracken, were brighter in the sunshine, and sometimes opalescent, all merging into each other, purple and blue and green and gold. We never met a soul, and the air was perfectly still. I have never been in such a dream-like place, all grey with mist, and these colours everywhere. Not a bird moved, and all the sound was the dripping of the mist. We came at last through Rogate and into South Harting at 3 o'clock, furiously hungry. Mrs Linlote said 'Well, I've just taken a rabbit pie from the oven, would you care for some of that', and I am sure our eyes glistened with rapture for we were just famished. We ate half the pie by the fire, while her little boy of 2 played about and showed us his toys, and ate up all the lumps of sugar I put in his train for people, and Rags ate and ate too – he had biscuits and bread and gravy. We had wanted to get from Rogate by train, but could not, so walked home, but food and rest and our own society made the 7 miles home go very fast and we got home just before 6, happy and not too tired. I had enjoyed it, and am not a bit stiff today, and all the better for Irene's company and the exertion and the change. The children had been happy too. Dr Hodson had called – bother him – thinking it was last weekend you were coming home. I shan't want him any way, though perhaps you'll be glad to see him.

So all your Hope has gone, and *now* perhaps you'll manage to work up a little enthusiasm about seeing me, and the children. Your poem was very pretty and apt, the children were very struck with it. Bronwen says, 'When Dicky grows up, he *thinks* he will be a poet, but he's not quite sure.'

We were up with the lark this morning, and Merfyn ran off to school all eagerness. I saw Irene off at Petersfield, and cycled back to Bronwen with Rags running behind. It *is* muddy now, and Rags is coated with it. I'll have to bath him before you return.

The foxes barked all night on the hills. I wonder if our way of expressing ourselves sounds melancholy to animals. The foxes' call, sounding when all else is still, and far away in the dark woods, sounds so terribly miserable and forsaken, just like a human sob does, yet I suppose he's feeling at his best ready for the fight with his rival, ready for the She fox when he has won her.

Milne *is* a beast, I think he must dislike you. Never mind, nothing matters so long as you are so well and happy, falling in love with girls with bell ropes of hair, and writing your books so easily, and playing animal grab – I used to know it but have forgotten it – and writing verses in albums. Oh dear you are so very well, that I don't believe you've ever spent an evening wishing, wishing, wishing that you were at home, and I spend all mine wishing you were here or I there. It is you men who are having the good time anyway, and before you return for good I want you to promise me a week end – a day or two with you there at the cottage. Or would I spoil it; but still it would only be for a day or two, and for me it would be glorious to be with you and the sea.

Miss Borsch[1] has not come back, but there is a new teacher in her place 'who knows about curves' Merfyn says. Can she have left I wonder. I'n not surprised, for she was discontented last term, but I'm sorry, for I think she was splendid for the children. But she may only be detained.

Baby and I went to fetch Merfyn from school today. We watched him play football, and kick the first goal. He was tired tonight – probably the first day he feels it rather, the walk and the work, and the games all helping, all the excitement of beginning again.

Harry and Janet are going to a dance at the Balter's where everyone is to dress in a peasant's dress; so Janet has borrowed the pedlar's smock of me, and a pair of grey stockings for Harry, and a sunbonnet for herself as milkmaid. She says they like you very much at Minsmere, and are delighted with your nice manners and looks. I knew they would like you, and I wish I were there to see it for myself, and drink in the pleasure of it. Nothing gives me such delight as to see people loving and admiring you. But I make you vain, and myself more and more sick for a sight of you.

So goodnight. I'm sorry to bother you, but I must tell you in case you think I've been careless of money, that I've not spent a penny on anything unnecessary, for it's only by dint of the most careful economy that I've been able to quite pay off my Xmas bills; also I've had all Merfyn's boots and slippers and Baby's too repaired, and that's cost a lot. Stamps and parcels have been expensive. I shan't have a penny left after paying Mrs Read for her work and some eggs. After that you'll wish me away, so goodnight and farewell, and come soon for I do want you, and am ever and wholly yours

Helen

ETC

1   A Swiss teacher at Bedales.

19: *To Edward*

Wednesday morning   *Ashford*
Just after breakfast
22 January 1908

Sweetheart, there is no one in the world, no one any way who is worth anything who has not a legion of devils, and now this misty morning you will know that I have, and that they have succeeded in making you unhappy. Nothing that any of those people you mention could tell me, nothing that you could tell me, no amount of devils would matter to me, you would always be the same to me. I do not love you because of your goodness, but because of the badness and goodness and light and darkness, because it all makes you, and you have taken my heart, and my body and my soul, and I shall never want them back again. I could not live if you ever said 'I have too many devils, your heart and body and soul are not safe in my keeping, take them back again'. And what of me dear one, you who are so ready to accuse yourself, are not my devils powerful and evil, and have they not shown themselves to you many times – this morning did not my letter fill the whole morning with misery for you. It is I that ask you to forgive me. I wanted you to be able to say when you came home how good I'd been and patient and cheerful, and now I shall not have the praise that would have meant heaven for me. We spoil our own joys, and those of the ones we love. And then it is bitter repentance, and then it is that love comes in and makes good out of bad, and light out of darkness. So make me good dear friend, and lover and husband, with the love you gave me long ago, and tell me what I can do to take away the unhappiness I have made for you.

The mist is clearing away, and such a blue sky is showing, and there is a bird on the top of the tree singing. I wish I could come to you just to kiss you dear and say I am sorry; for now I am good and calm and only eager for your coming for all to be well. I don't expect I can get away. Janet writes to ask me to put it off till the following week, and the 28th I suppose that would be, as her father is coming to town on the 21st. And I won't do that, I want you too much to willingly postpone your coming a day, an hour.

So I'm quite happy now, it doesn't matter so much as I thought it did, and if I can come to town that will be a fine treat to be with you and Mac, and sometime later perhaps Janet will let us go down for a week end – just you and I. Let it be like that.

Merfyn is very well, and so is Bronwen, though yesterday she did not seem quite herself. But she woke up in the night and said 'I feel as jolly as a lobster' and so she must be all right I'm sure. Anyway this morning she *is* quite well and looks well and everything. If she does have measles it would not be wise for you to come, but she won't I feel sure.

Am I forgiven sweetheart, I mean are you happy again, for it is your spirit I have hurt and if that is well then it is well with me too. I have such a lot to make up for that the fortnight shall not be wasted, no not one hour of it in sadness. The devils have had their fling, it will be no hard matter to keep them imprisoned, and when you come – Oh we shall be very happy, shan't we, and if we could get a little extra week end it would be perfect, but anyway it will be perfect being together again.

Here is the paper. I did not understand you wanted it as well as the large notebook.

Thanks for the cheque.

Let me kiss you. The children are well and happy and longing for you. Today in bed they were saying in order the men they liked best. 'Daddy, Ivor, Rags' were the first on Baby's list. Merfyn's began with Daddy, though it did not go on so nobly, falling down to Gappa and Uncle Julian.

Farewell now dearest. I feel strong now and well and happy. Forget today. Goodbye. Ever and wholly I am yours

Helen

I hope the paper is right. It is all I can find. Everything is well, you understand.

ETC

20: *To Edward*

Wednesday night,   *Berryfield Cottage*
22 January 1908

Dearest one, I hope and hope there will be no letter for me tomorrow, that you will not write until Thursday when you will have what I hope will comfort you.

This is only to say goodnight and farewell, till you come to me and the children who do so long for you.

I can't imagine now that I was so lately miserable, selfish, whining. I'm tired tonight, but sad no longer, only longing for you to come when all will be well.[1]

Merfyn was out in the warm sun today, and Bronwen is quite well and as happy as ever. Oh sweetheart I wish I had not made you feel so bitter, I would do anything to undo it all. I do love you dear however I seem not to, and nothing that the worst devil in you could tell me would make a bit of difference. I am perfectly content with you, my brain would think no ill of you; the more you told me the more I should feel you needed my love, and needing it it would be there for you.

Tell me you do need it dearest, as I always need your love.

I truly have been very very lonely; but would you have me always always happy and content away from you. And loneliness and depression got into my brain – not my heart at all – and put words there that had no thoughts with them, and I wrote them and gave you pain, when all my desire is to give you joy. I forgot all the delight I had stored up, but now I have it all before me, and I am like a tired traveller who has found a cool green field with shade and stream to rest by. I want to comfort you, but words which came easily to hurt you, are powerless now, I feel they are almost mute now that I desire to comfort you. My body is for your comfort and delight, and I wish I might hold you in my arms, and kiss your eyes and your forehead and your dear hands.

I have told Janet it does not matter, and asked her if we can have the cottage for a week end later.

I will come to meet you in town, so tell me when you will come.

Tell me too that the bitterness I gave you I have taken away, and that you love me. I am ever and wholly yours

   Helen

ETC

1 HT very rarely wrote letters of complaint (see *Edward Thomas. A Portrait*, Chapter 9). Merfyn and then Bronwen got the measles, so ET did not go home (except for one night) until March. HT spent the last weekend of February with him at Minsmere.

21: *To Helen*

Dearest one

Just a word before I go to bed at 11. After writing to the children and you it was nearly 6.30 and I lit a pipe and walked out slowly along a not too steep road out of Tregaron, with the river winding near and below me. The mist of the day had increased and the sky was misted over and the wind had dropped. So I really could walk slowly and all my restlessness was gone, nor did I think about anything. On a little steep rocky hill just above an end of the town some girls were singing songs together, songs I did not know, intermittently and running about. It was getting dark when I sat down above the river and looked at it and the late birds flitting about. Hardly anyone was on the road. Then I got up and went further on still very slowly and there were still people at work in the fields or on the haystacks. A boy galloped after some cows. A girl was singing in a farmyard. A distant bull bellowed. A train went by. But it was very silent and I was very happy. I did not turn back until it was quite dark and even then I was able to keep to my slow pace and without thought until I got back. Then I made a few notes and read a scene of Richard the Second and it was dinner time. Since then with Arthur I have been in a different world, but now he is gone to bed I am back in the other world and must say goodnight to you in it. Goodnight. I hope all is well.

Thursday

Arthur and I have both been out all day together up at that mountain lake again. It was another fine day with hot moments when I could lie down in the sun. Arthur was unsuccessful again. I tried a little but hadn't the patience and I strolled about and sat down most of the time. Then we were lucky in getting a 4 mile lift home from a farmer's son who knows Mr. Rowland. We are only just back at 8.30 on a perfect evening of cloudless but misty sky with a few bright stars and a crescent moon that has changed from white to red as we drove down. Now we are to have supper and then I must pack up my things and put some in a parcel for the wash.

Now it is after supper – I have paid my bill – and am waiting for bed and to pack my things. I am afraid I can't write a letter. I was expecting the parcel from you, but perhaps you sent it to Swansea. But I shall look for it by tomorrow first post just before I leave at 9. I must go now.

Goodbye and my love to Mother and the children all. I am ever and wholly yours Edwy.

NLW

1 ET was walking in Wales for ten days, here with Arthur Hardy, a close friend from schooldays, who later paid the Thomases many visits when on leave from the South African Police.

22: *To Edward*

Dearest one

I do hope your day has been as happy as mine. I have just put my family to bed and I think they all felt the day had been satisfactory all round. Of course they did not say so, that would have spoilt it all; but all were so eager to talk to me of their plans for tomorrow and of their interests – all seemed so excited and eager and happy together that after I had a chat with each in bed, I felt sorry to leave them and come down to my solitude.

The warm weather has been nice. Windy and not sunny all the time, but still warm and pleasant, and the children have been out of doors all day long, and I a good part of the day. Baby,[1] who has joined in the unusual happiness has been especially jolly and happy. She slept three hours on the terrace today, and when she woke she lay in her perambulator saying softly to herself 'Mama Mama'. Of course all morning we were watching for Ernest and Florrie, and I had prepared for them, but much to our disappointment they did not come.

After dinner the boys went into the wood where they have built a wigwam; and Edith took Baby and Bronwen out as well, Margaret preferring to stay and garden with me. So we sowed the Sheiling poppy seeds and the sunflower seeds – the latter very carefully in boxes, and then went down into the woods to the boys who we pounced upon with yells and war whoops as they were busy with their hut.

Then Bronwen came racing down to us full of the news of a wren's nest she had found all by herself, and eager to tell you at once on her 'best' postcard. She'd forgot to tell you she'd seen a swallow too. So then we all went in to tea, and after tea played card games (after I had put Baby to bed) till bed time. They now do not bath at night but in the mornings. This gives a little extra time between tea and bed, which is very much appreciated.

Boots have been oiled and jobs done. Merfyn is not very grand. He's got a horrid cough, but still with Dicky he's found plenty to do, I hope to get him by degrees to take little or no sugar, for according to one's local authority he has all the signs of too much sugar. But I don't want to enforce it now. I don't want it to be so conscious on his part, and also not to make it a grievance with him.

It is extraordinary the way Lupton[2] echoes his wife – and yet not very either: he has thought out very little himself and she evidently is a very strong character. She by the way thinks I am a wonderfully healthy looking woman and says my tongue shows a really wonderfully clean inside – the rougher the tongue the better the interior condition.

Lupton has not got a wheelbarrow for sale, but says old Cendewood makes good ones. He soon starts the Bedales job, and yesterday went to Norfolk to look at timber.

The terrace is *lovely*, and my cherished blue gentian is almost out. Mary comes on Thursday, and I am looking forward to her visit very much.

The poor law meeting was good, *very*, but a very small audience, though select, and there was a good deal of discussion, and Mr Fordham and Miss Lowndes got at log-a-heads, but the Vicar in the chair was very discreet and clever at his job, and all went off well.

If I were you I could tell of such a day as this has been and make you feel wherein lies its beauty for me. Cooking for my big family, having Baby murmur Mama to herself, working with Margaret in the garden, pouncing on the boys in the wood, seeing Bronwen running eagerly down the steps to tell me her find, and that she had written her postcard to you. Feeding Baby with her orange and talking to her, and feeling too that I am so well and have so much milk for her, and then the games with the children, and a nice talk that we had about Rags and they said '*Can't* you think of anything else about him, we do so love it.'

No indeed, hope has not left me, nor joy, nor real living. I feel rich in all the things worth having and can give and give. So take what I have as with my milk, the more Baby has the more flows in, so with all that I feel tonight, the more I give to you, the more you take from me, the more I have.

Goodnight now. I have a lot of sewing to do and of late I have been working till 12 o'clock. The children do love you very truly,

so see the love and kisses, and I am ever and wholly yours
   Helen
   Some of Mater's of course.

ETC

1 Helen Elizabeth Myfanwy Thomas was born on 16 August 1910.
2 Geoffrey Lupton, a furniture-maker and disciple of William Morris, built a house called Wick Green for the Thomases, which they rented from him. With its adjacent 'study' and large garden, it is close to the ET memorial stone above Steep.

23: *To Edward*

Dearest one

I am all alone at 8.30 after giving the children their half weekly bath and trying to get Baby after to sleep, she being worried by spots. I, having nothing handy to cool them with, put my finger in my mouth and moistened them with my spit, and I was surprised to see her imitate me, even sleepy as she was.

This note is just as a comfort to myself after a hot burning day, though after your letter a happy one. The big room which I have let the children run wild in as anyway we could not use it, is being cleaned tomorrow so I am preparing it, sorting out the newspapers etc. and clearing away rubbish of all sorts and generally making order out of chaos.

Merfyn took Baby to the 2 o'clock post, but apparently that does not reach you first thing as I thought it would. This evening I played with the children in the lane, Baby in her pram laughing at our doings. It is strange how running and jumping amuse her. Then when she was in bed, Merfyn and I weeded. I think the garden now is clear of weeds. We've got up an enormous pile, mostly prickly thistles, not a lot of any thistledown. Lupton says we ought to begin digging the potatoes, which the dry weather is making to sprout again. So Merfyn and I will begin that job before breakfast tomorrow. That's a job I like very much. It's not time to dig up any of the root vegetables yet Lupton says. He says there's nothing to be done to that drain but to flush it out every now and then and with some carbolic in the water.

Irene I heard for the first time is at Southwold having a lovely time, but they move from there today, and she gives me her address so that I can write to ask her advice about the bastard. From the letter I rather gathered they wanted to find a home for the child with people who would be glad to have him as a gift, and no more communication on either side. But of course I may be mistaken. I would much rather have a girl I think; but I think the question is too serious to be discussed on paper.

You've been away a fortnight tomorrow. How long it seems. I do want you, but I fear your coming almost as much as I long for it. I always hope for and expect so much. I have the house garnished and the garden free of weeds, and then expect it always to be like that, with everyone beaming and happy. But we are not figures on a Grecian urn. And because the weeds grow up again, and the house gets untidy, and because it is life we are living and not posing for the delight of poets, I get horrid shocks which I can never prepare myself for old as I am.

Oh do come back and be happy with me once more. I'm sick to death of the loneliness eating my heart out with anxieties and lost hopes. But don't come till the rain comes. I have a superstitious feeling that with the rain good will come all round. This drought is unnatural and unkind, though I do love the sun and the blue sky of it. But the rain and the sweet smell of wet earth would bring I feel relief to the soul of me. So dearest stay away as long as you can, and come striding home with a jolly 'cooee' for us across the valley and three children in your arms all of a bustle, and a kiss for me when they give us a moment, and then a meal, and a long evening of calm talk. That is my picture. Oh let it all come true! Or is it like the washing in the Jordan, difficult because of its simplicity?

Goodnight now sweetheart. I hope you are at Amanford and liking it.

Goodnight, ever and wholly yours / Helen

This £1 clears me out almost. I am just going down to enquire about the sticks. That fool Spiers has made a muddle of it somehow.

So thankful all is well with you. Here too it is well and better and better as I learn good news of you. Bronwen looks for another letter.

NLW

24: *To Edward*

Sunday night, September 1911   *Wick Green*

Dearest one

Only just a hurried note after a busy day. All is well and I hope with you it is so too. The weather is perfect for walking. A light cool wind and bright sun, but Oh for rain. There is no news at all. We work in the house and the garden and go walks and play with Myfanwy.

Tonight Lupton made me furious. He saw he had, but I won't tell you of it just now. It was only his absolutely brutal speech which I hate him for. I was digging potatoes, and the children seeing something was amiss went and picked me a lot of large ripe blackberries, which cured me quickly, bless them. Tonight all alone I have been reading Davies' poems, and then sleeping till Edith came in.

Bronwen was pleased with her letter. She *ever* loves you that child. She talks of you a lot and wishes for your return. Today on a walk she and I were talking of you, and Baby listening said 'Dada, Dada' and looked about. She also says 'Down Denal' in a stern voice.

The *Saturday* came not the *Eyewitness*. I wrote to the woman about the child, setting out all my good qualities for fitness to stepmother the poor little boy, but I suspect my terms are too high.

I'm glad the sticks came. I did write the address on a tie-on label *and* on the brown paper covering. Thank you for the 15/-. I love that walk to Carreg Cennen and think of you there and in other parts of those walks you and I took. I wonder shall we ever be there together again. I hope from the hills will come peace, and that you will return home with some for me. I too have need of it.

Well I must go now to bed, to get up early. Merfyn gets up early every day to dig potatoes.

Goodnight and farewell sweetheart. Ever and wholly I am yours

Helen.

ETC

25: *To Edward*

Friday, 16 December 1911   *Wick Green*

Dearest one,

Only a few lines hoping this finds you as it leaves me at present, very well thank you!

There is no news except that there are only four days to your homecoming. And when you get this there'll only be three, unless you count Tuesday as 31 days. It will seem a month of wet Sundays, from getting up time till starting off to meet you time. The children and I may meet you, that is if I can find time. I daresay I'll stroll down to the station, but if I am not here, I daresay I shall have gone to the McTaggarts to tea, so in case I am otherwise enjoyed I've told Maud to make tea for you, though if you like to wait supper till 7.30 or 8 I'll be sure to be home then. The McTaggarts are so very nice, and have asked me to go, and as *nothing* is happening on Tuesday after all the gaieties of the term I thought it would be a good opportunity.

I cannot answer your two last loving lovely letters, it's no good trying. I did not get *too* wet and cold in the hailstorm, but I'm very grateful all the same for the warmth and cheeryness of the sun after it. You see it's intoxicating me somehow. I'll be as mad as ten hatters by Tuesday if this sort of thing goes on.

I'll air your clothes for you, and get out the sweater and the old mac. (There's some wedding cake for you which I did not send on.) I've put the notebooks in your letter chest, and locked it. I paid the bills and have got the receipts. Baring wants £8 all at a fell swoop, but it was a glorious debauch of bill paying and receipts reaping.

The children go to Bedales tonight with the School to see *The Midsummer Night's Dream*. They won't be out till 9 o'clock, and of course I shall be there to meet them. I'll keep the books hidden.

I'm so glad that old Borrow is done and that we are a yard or so further from the workhouse. I'm not sorry you have left Llaugharne.[1] Those singing, running, pale girls with creamery voices who pass the windows of hardworking handsome young married men 50 times a day don't do it for nothing I'll be bound. Oh no. You're better at home with your old woman, who once ran and who once passed your windows as often as she could, and sang too when she'd a mind to, but who was never pale nor creamery (not that I think much of either quality in young girls), but who kissed you before you kissed her (was it yesterday?) Cream or no cream girls are pretty much the same all the world over, and I'd not give a snap of the finger for one of them passing your window while you are bending over your Borrow (forsooth). Sit there with one eye perhaps on your book, but the other wanton eye looking for cream and roses and not what, while the huzzies pass before you that you may the more rove after them. Even so, the hailstones may have got into my heart, but if they did the warmth and foolishness they found there soon changed them into magic wine 'which maketh glad the heart of man'. Well, don't expect me at Petersfield will you. Oh, but do expect Myfanwy who I daresay will go by *herself* on *her own two legs.*

For yesterday at the Bedfords she walked from Molly Bedford to me with a delicious little chuckle of delight and pride, and then again a step or two. Oh but she's lovely, and now she says Daddy not Dada, and Mammy not Mama, and everything she says is perfect. She's the very spit of her mother isn't she? Bless her rosy cheeks and her bright eyes and her voice when she sings very high notes.

Not a single line or word till Tuesday. I'm so excited about my tea party at the McTaggarts. It will be jolly won't it? Give my love to Mother, and tell Julian I'm sorry he can't come and kiss your father for me, because I must let out somehow and that seems to me quite a good way. Good luck in town, and the best of luck at home, and a *sensible* wife, not the scatter brain creature I half expect you've got.

Any way such as she is she's yours,
Helen

ETC

1 ET stayed in Laugharne from 1 November to 17 December, completing *George Borrow.*

26: *To Helen*

16 August 1912   *Selsfield House*
                                                                    [*East Grinstead*]

Dearest one

Here we are waiting for Ellis to turn up.[1] We have been over the garden with Mrs. Ellis and down the deep dark ghyll where they quarried the sandstone hundreds of years ago, now full of hazel and oak. The Ellises are thinking of adding a newer bit to their garden – a square deep hollow with sandmartin's nests and ragwort, suitable for an outdoor theatre, fives court etc. It is drizzling now, but there is a wood fire in the big open fireplace and Mervyn is deep in cushions and the *Chronicle*. Our lodgings last night were a great success. We had eggs and fruit for breakfast and only paid 5/- for everything. The people are named Wadey, and if I go to Slinfold again I shall go there.

Ellis arrived at 6 and cut this short. Mervyn sat down and listened to us talking till dinner at 7.30 when he went to bed with a bath.

Well, about Friday, we were again in a district of parks tho we did not see so many grand entrances, iron gates, stone pillars surmounted by eagles or suits of armour with no men inside as at Petworth. First we went to see Shelley's house, Field Place, but only saw that it was there among trees near Broadbridge Heath, a small treeless roadside common halfway to Horsham, with reeds, and a pub nearby called the 'Dog and Bacon' with a big sign of a dog up on a chair sniffing at some bacon that stands beside a mug of beer on a table – obviously the original of Worthington's 'what is it master likes so much' except that here the dog is facing right, which is harder to draw then left.

We didn't stay long in Horsham which has a square called Carfax as at Oxford. We kept some way on the Brighton road passing close to a beautiful lily mill pond at Whitesbridge in a dark hollow. We turned off at Manning's Heath, which is like Ashdown, a big region of oak and fir woods cloven by deep valleys, several containing big long ponds – one a Hammer Pond used in the ironworks when wood instead of coal supplied the furnaces and Sussex was almost as black as Staffordshire. Some of the

Forest is high and bare and purple for acres with heather and their undulations against a background of wood are lovely. Our road was horseless for a long way, with barbed wire to keep us out of the heather stretches in the east but no hedge on the west where there was oak birch bracken and heather – heather only at the sunny edge. We sat and looked at the view, the barbed wire and our bicycles. Isn't Coolhurst a nice name? It is a house with a small park and entrance gates just South of Horsham. The nicest flower all the way was the wood betony at the edges of the woods. It looks so wise – a purple flower like basil, but darker, with dark leaves, rather stiff. The combination of oak birch bracken heather and harebell is one of the sweetest.

Then we got to a main road which took us to Crawley – an automobile-yellow town where we bought fruit and which we ate a few miles farther on after going into Worth churchyard, a big rough place full of Brookers, Streeters, Ellis, Morris, Davis, Rice etc., entombed among many trees of yew and lime etc. The church, which has a short Sussex spire and Saxon double windows, was shut. But where some men were cutting up larch wood in Worth Forest we ate our fruit and got to Ellis' at 3. Meantime my bicycle had gone wrong, and I now find I shall have to borrow Ellis' to finish the tour, as a cone in the back wheel is broken in half and it may be long before a new one comes from the maker.

Mervyn has gone to Cowden. We sit and smoke and talk.

Thank you for your letter. I hope this is not too dull a return for it.

Goodbye I am ever and wholly yours Edwy

Please keep these letters

ETC

1 ET and Merfyn were on a cycling holiday, but ET also spent periods in 1913–14 as a paying guest at the home of Vivian Locke Ellis, a wealthy poet, dilettante editor and antiques-dealer.

27: *To Helen*

Friday, 15 November 1912   *32 Rue des Vignes, Paris*

Dearest

Thank you for your letter (*not* enclosing Guthrie's).[1] I wish you had come. But it isn't that I put the children before you but that I put the *comfort of my own imagination* before you. With you here, I should have had more confidence. However I have now bought several things, hired taxis, etc. You should have heard me asking for Castor Oil which the chemist did not know by that name – it is Huile de Ricin. Well I got it. I am sorry to say I need it. And I was yesterday disabled by an instep so full of ache that I could hardly put it to the ground. I am afraid this is connected with the wine and the increased amount of meat, and the condition of my stomach. So I am now eating only nuts, fruit, and bread and butter.

I went to the Luxembourg Gallery in the morning and looked chiefly at the statuary. It's quite a small gallery and yet crowded and too full for one to do more than pick out what one would like to steal. From there I walked to the river, found my way across it and up many streets to Jones' office.[2] We had lunch. Mrs Jones met us after and she and I went to the Opera Comique and saw *La Traviata*. Well done, but stupid. I can't get over the stupidity of acting and singing together. But there was a dance of five minutes. About 12 slender girls doing a very simple high kicking, low bending in and out dance, with pretty oriental costumes to the knee, tied like a towel so as to display the behind, scarlet stockings, and shoes, and green drawers occasionally visible. They had small really pretty faces and hair down and smiled without any of the hideous effects of paint on which English choruses often show. $3^1/_2$ hours of it with my sore foot never forgettable was too much. We had tea and went back at 6 when I read till 8 o'clock dinner. Jones not returning till 9. In the evening we talked about Hootons etc, about poverty and boasting of poverty when you can't boast of anything else. Jones played the pianola till nearly 12. Then I slept till 7.30. I sleep very well in these darkened rooms. Every window in Paris has thin iron shutters which are locked at night against thieves.

I have the same objection to the tiny cottage as you and should be glad to try the Powell's if you like, especially if you could do without a servant. Also I am certain it need not prevent you from going away as often as you do now. Have you heard more from the Russels or Powells?

I think it was Miss *Wilson* had the waterproof. And did you get the address; and will you give it me?

Mrs Anthony hasn't written, though I wrote and perhaps you did. Nor has Rhys,[3] in fact only 2 out of 8 people I wrote to before starting. De la Mare wrote on Monday to Rusham Road, offering Monday and Thursday – had mislaid my letter – was too much rushed – said nothing else. As I had sent a postcard from here explaining why I didn't appear if he has suggested it, there was nothing to be said. I am sorry to lose him, but I am sure I can't keep him by making all the efforts to bring off meetings myself, while he does nothing.

The weather continues grey and drizzly and coldish, as it is with you apparently. Today I shall only be able to get about in cabs and trains. I shall go to the Louvre, I think, and look about for some presents. I have now seen the streets almost as crowded and noisy as London and less under control. They keep to the *right* too which adds to difficulties. The crowd is mostly men and women. Very few girls 17–22 because they don't get about much and never alone. It makes a lot of difference. Of course you see young servants, but not many. The servants here go about in the streets bareheaded. I suppose because I haven't been about after dark much, I haven't seen any recognisable prostitutes.

My hosts are extremely kind. They will do or obtain anything I want at home or elsewhere and show no uneasiness at my ways. This afternoon Mrs Jones will take me to a place where I may find a birthday present for Father and something for Mother perhaps.

By the way will you send my evening dress and the best white shirt you can find (from the bottom of the chest) to Rusham Road in case I don't go to Rhys and can get to the Nation. Send it off in good time on Monday with the white scarf you will see in the chest, and put any gold studs you can find with the shirt. If however all the shirts are limp I must borrow from Julian.

Goodbye, and thank you for everything, for typewriting for example. I hope you are not having to force yourself to write so sweetly to me. I hope all is well. I am ever and wholly yours
Edwy
Saturday (16.11.12) P.S. Will you keep my Paris letters because I have been very careless with notes.

1   James Guthrie, artist, writer, editor; friend of ET and of Bottomley. He first published a few of ET's poems under the pseudonym 'Eastaway'.
2   ET suddenly went to Paris for a week, staying with the Joneses. A friend and one-time colleague of Harry Hooton, S. Jones was British representative at a French bank.
3   Ernest Rhys, editor of the Everyman series to which ET contributed six volumes.

28: *To Helen*

Saturday, 16 November 1912   *32 Rue des Vignes, Paris*

Dearest,

Went to Opera for *Meistersingers*. The music enchanted *and* bored me. The play at least was very boring. The convention of opera is too much for me.

My problem today is to get something for Mervyn. Goodbye. Both Jones' insist you must come with me next time. We must try to arrange it.

I am all yours
Edwy

Sunday, 17 in the evening to Gaiete Lyrique Theatre – saw *The Magic Flute*. It was lovely all through, never interfering with the music and the music always music and often culminating in sweet melodies. The women were either fat or gross but the voices were splendid and the dresses choice and varied. I could have stood a night of it. It is such a relief after Wagner's ponderous pretentious barbarous German magnificence.

I wish the children could have heard Mozart. They would have liked every moment of it.

If I had stayed a month here I could have got quite at home in French. Mrs J left me at the stores yesterday and I went about getting the various somethings I wanted and even ostentatiously quarrelled over my change, though I was in the wrong. Well I have to leave soon after 7 tomorrow and I hope I can get a good night.

Probably I shall ask the Freemans[1] for the next weekend or the one afterwards. I have got Mrs F something to console her for being put off last week. But I shall want to work – I haven't thought of my fiction since I left London.[2] Goodbye dearest and Mervyn and Bronwen and Baby. I am all yours Edwy

---

[1]   John Freeman, poet, critic and member of the Poetry Bookshop group. He helped to see *Poems* of 'Edward Eastaway' (1917) through the press.
[2]   He was writing *The Happy-Go-Lucky Morgans* (1913).

29: *To Helen*

Monday, 23 June 1913   *Broughton Gifford, Wilts.*

Dearest

Is there anything in particular you would like me to get for your birthday – anything, for instance, for the cottage? I put this first in case I forget.

It is now nearly 3. Clifford[1] left at 12 for London. It has been quite a pleasant time. Yesterday afternoon we strolled in the river and I bathed. I bathed again this morning just before the rain came on at 8. It has been wet and hot alternatively. There was a young actor named Elvey (né Levy, I suspect) here for the weekend. But we managed to talk a great deal and I did very much as liked, and slept etc. well. I have read through the French book on Jefferies. It is a crib from me from beginning to end, quite openly and with many compliments as penetrating, philosophic etc. It will not be easy to write an article on it.

This afternoon I shall perhaps go to Dillybrook and look round and have tea and find the forwarded letters on my return I hope – thanks for your telegram. Tomorrow I shall start after breakfast if fine: if not I shall wait about and if it keeps wet go to Salisbury mostly by train and hope for the fine weather on Wednesday. I shall return by Bramdean and if the children are *not* at home and you have time you might meet me there at 3.30 to 4. I shall return past the 'George' and along the Winchester road and up by Froxfield Green. I hope things look well for the move and that there was no difficulty with Mother.[2]

It is delicious here now, some fields pale, the hay carried in, some covered with 'roads' and cocks, many unmown full of clover, birdsfoot trefoil, marguerite and knapweed and sorrel. In the morning you hear the starlings in the hayfields and the corncrakes at night. A heron was very much surprised to find me at the river before him this morning. There are some golden lilies in the river and white comfrey everywhere and roses and honeysuckle and flag flowers in the moat at Great Thalfidd manor house. The long grass bends over the path and wets your legs. The paths are *dark* green across the pale hay-fields. The garden is full of larkspur, pinks, snapdragons, canterbury bells purple

68

and white. It is blowing strong form the west but shining bright. The elder hedge in the garden is caked over with blossom. I am alone here with the silent Emma and the ghosts of five voices and dancers with 'scuffing' feet in the hall and a girl with a middle size giltedged tray all trembling which a man who stayed here 40 years ago says he saw. He swore it, putting his hand in the ground and calling on God to fix it there if he was lying – he lifted it up triumphantly like a conjuror. This was yesterday by the river. But at night I only dreamt the D.C. had chucked me at my own request and I was in a state between pride and despair. *Will you* keep this letter for me, to save me copying it out?

Later.

Thank you ever so much for your jolly letter. I *was* glad to find it when I got back from Dillybrook where everyone asked after you. They were all well, haymaking. I had tea and watched a white cock and the white turkey cock fighting. The cock bent his head, fluffed out his neck feathers in a huge ruff and then jumped together. But the cock always had to give back and the turkey always advanced and nearly succeeded in standing on him. After a time the cock's only way of avoiding flight was to slip *under* the turkey when the turkey was half treading on him: then he took to walking round the turkey and refusing to retreat again got trodden on. When the turkey knew he was victor he scraped his outspread wing-quills along the ground and paraded with the long trench all blue and swollen over his beak and the dark sporran of hairs conspicuous in the middle of his chest. The cock walked slowly away. They were quite silent.

We got back late at 6.45 and have no time for a letter. As things are – the Lord be thanked – perhaps I had better not expect you on Wednesday: all the same I shall come that way at the time I said.

About cases, I want 4 for sending things to Thorp[3] and Rusham Road. Please order them of Fuller.

Can you get Lupton in for Wednesday to talk things over. There's no need to have the garden dug before we move. I shan't mind. Or if I do I can clear out.

Would you like the Farjeons[4] here next weekend? If so write

69

a note at once to

Eleanor Farjeon, 137 Fellows Road, South Hampstead.

Why doesn't Mrs King print me in the Vineyard then? Eh? Ask her.

Now I must go. I've had to correct a proof and time is close. I am ever and wholly your Edwy.

Give the children kisses from me and Mother too if she's not gone. I hope something has transpired.

NLW

1 Clifford Bax, editor, dramatist, theosophist, brother of the composer Arnold Bax.
2 The Thomases moved from Wick green to Yew Tree Cottage in the village of Steep on 23 July 1913.
3 Thorp, a bookseller, bought all of ET's unwanted review copies.
4 See Eleanor Farjeon, *Edward Thomas, The Last Four Years* (1958; 1997).

30: *To Helen*

Dearest

I hope all is well. I heard nothing from you yesterday or this morning. All here is well. It is now 11 a.m. and after an afternoon talk with Gordon (who is still spending his days in bed) I am going to write to you instead of making notes.

The weather is perfect, hot and misted, the hills and sea and also the small mountainous clouds all softly misted. But then a SW wind rustling the sycamore and hazel and oak and pine and bracken all round them. The house is a comfortable villa inside very neat and pretty, outside just 1880 or so, and made quite tolerable by ivy and honeysuckle. It has windows everywhere that look through the low surrounding trees (as old as the house) over a wonderful series of views, lesser and greater hills, the lesser often covered with woods up to their ridges and with parklike meadows running up to the bays at their edges; but the farther hills showing much bare limestone among bushes or grass, though clumped with firs; some are scarred with bare pale quarries. A mile away below under a gentle slope of stones and scattered trees is the lake I bathed in this morning, Hawes Water, half a mile long and a quarter broad, with pennon-leafed sedges standing in the shallows all round – silversanded shallows with very tiny white shells, very soft when you walk and in fact letting you in up to your knees until suddenly there is a drop into deep water with loose weeds that don't come up to the surface and there you plunge in and swim to another white shore where there is a gap in the sedges. It was delicious at 7.30: the bank I bathed from being rough flat pasture with thyme and eyebright among stones and many birdseye primroses which are like small red campions clustered at top of a straight thin stem about a foot high with a rosette of little leaves on the ground (I can hear the cuckoo now singing quite perfectly and unbrokenly far off over the stony high land on which the house is.) Also a lot of yellow rockrose everywhere. It grows on the roadsides with marguerites. The pink and the white wild roses are out, and the elder and stonecrop. The rockrose is best where it grows round the corrugated whitish and sandy gray limestone that occupies more than half the surface of the land here; and in places the rockrose seems to be growing on the stone itself. Emily [Bottomley] met me and took me by a short cut to the house which is on a hilltop by itself, on all sides approached over slippery tussocks of turf and stone mixed with thorn and briers and bracken. The house is only cut off from this by a stone wall and its trees, hardly any garden: most of the land inside the wall is the same as outside, stony and grassy, only with thicker bushes, bramble and bracken and trees, often hiding and overtopping the wall. (It is lovely to hear the cuckoo's voice in the mist quite unspoilt. There is also some hawthorn blossom only just past its prime.) There is juniper on the hillside, but very little of it, the palest and the blackest green mixed. Behind me in the West at the window is a little bay in the Morecambe Bay edged with misty hills, and near is Silverdale church tower and scattered white or grey farms and villas among the woods which can't always cover the pale stone. The trees are mostly oak and ash. If it were clear the flatbottomed valley between the woodedhills that I see running north – the Valley of Kent – would lead up to the higher mountains lying in a semicircle far inland: also eastward I should see Ingleborough. But at present I prefer the pale-dark woods and the pale but not chalky stones misted over and the far-off cuckoo and the near willow wren and the wind dryly rustling.

The railway journey after Leeds was very pleasant. I had been coolish for the first hour or so and I even put on my overcoat. But at Leeds at 3.30 I changed into a slow train going through Keighley and over the moors to Carnforth, a much better way than the way I've been before through Wigan and Lancaster. Not very long after Leeds there were no more factories and the land began to rise and one could see its ups and downs of green with stone walls and strong rivulets and stone farms with ash trees; and ahead to the left high misty pale mountains through which the railway goes. Near a station beginning with CON and ending in EY there was such a nice stone house, ivycovered with windowless turrets at either side presumably for staircases, and a lower addition at both ends. [A sketch of the house is here added on the side.] Not very big. Perhaps three times as large as Elses

Farm, not more. The beauty of it was it stood at the top of a gentle but decided hill, with trees at the side but bare below the house front for the sake of the view across the railway to the low hills and mountains beyond. After this the railway (I imagine) climbed a great deal and the pastures were divided by blackish stone walls. The farms with gray stone roofs were fewer, the hillsides stonier and barer. In fact many walls had no trees at all, only here and there was a plantation or by a house a few ashes, and then were bigger and barer hills with scars of rocks behind the near ones. We stopped at stations by streams with thrushes singing in thorns and swallows skimming. It was hot but not too hot for you and me. There were dusky long-wooled sheep on the hillsides.

I read some of *The Idiot* and some of *Green Roads* and altogether enjoyed the journey, and when I found there was a lake as well as the sea to bathe in I wanted nothing else. I've had a bath before bed after supper, while the nightjar jarred about twenty yards away very strongly, the wind being still and the light dim. This has been a year of years for weather. I wish things were coming right. Still I have contrived to get more pleasure than almost ever before out of the weather. We have been happier too, in spite of all.

Will you *keep* this part of the letter and send it back to me?

ETC

31: *To Helen*

Friday, 9 October 1914   *Swansea*

Dearest

I got back again by hard riding in time for tea here at 4.30. I had promised to be in for dinner but it was such a fine day that when I left Gwili's at Amanford I planned a rather long way round. Well, I will tell you first about yesterday.

It was a dull morning and drizzled a little before 11 – I had promised Gwili to arrive about 3.30 by train if wet, otherwise by road. I was at first with John Williams on the sands.[1] It was beautiful. Sea and land hazy, the tide out, the sand rather dull brown and yellowish small stones some covered with green weed standing in shallow pools. JW was throwing stones into the sea for his eunuch dog Togo. I was watching a gull chasing a small sharpwinged sea bird over the stone, following its movement exactly but unable to pounce, till at last the small one settled suddenly and the gull went off. Out at sea stood the towered dredgers. On the sands 1/4 mile off some men were being drilled but not a sound could be heard from them. I started at 11 up out of the town towards the Caermarthen road – a fair surface but up and down – and was soon away from the coalpits between dusty hedges and rusty grass – often bracken in the hedges with knapweed flowers and some small dark purple scabious. I was thinking how far afield I could get before 3.30 and whether to call on Thomas at Pontardulais. However I ran into David John in the street so had to see Thomas and stayed to dinner and saw Blodwen and Kate[2] and the pigs, one to be killed in November when it would weigh 12 score. He has had plenty of apples (Newton Wonder and Peasgood Nonesuch) and pears and is sending us some *cabbage plants* next week; also plenty of caterpillars like us. They were getting a large quantity of butter in (so they were at Amanford), the best butter of the season, the cows having been in the aftermath: after this they will be having oil cake. so they were telling me why the Michaelmas goose is so good – because he eats the gleanings in the cornfields. (There is a proverb that the best goose is fed on the gleanings.) Thomas was full of the 'Herald' doctrine and furious against landowners and employers who press men to enlist. Tommy ought to go but he is doing well in the coal mines and passing exams, for a mining engineer.

Thomas came with me after dinner a mile out on the Forest road, the Caermarthen road, which I stuck to till I had to turn off to get to Amanford in time. There was a high road looking down on the steep Gwili valley and over hillsides with copses. The road itself had the best of mixtures in the hedges – oak hazel bramble and fern with knapweed and small scabious and some hawkweed. The prettiest thing was where the road is carried over the narrow steep Gwili valley, with the dark water pouring only just visible deep below through oak and ash and hazel and above all bare mountain ash full of the rich crimson branches – also a farm orchard came down to the stream with rosy apples. Then for 2 miles I had the Gwili and the oaks of its valley on my right near by. I turned off by a bad road full of colliers with red lips returning or standing about with newspapers – rusty oak fields in the beautiful low yellow hedges and red hips and barbed wire, and on the hill tops coalpit chimneys and the red fern of the Llynllochowel [*sic*] moorland. I had many steep descents down to little streams and white farms and up again. The pale green grass and dark rush was characteristic. I had had enough riding however when I got to Gwili's house. His wife and Nest (aged 2.8) and Gwenllian (aged 4 months) and Gwili were a very homely household, with scrappy delayed meals except the set tea with the silver in the best room among bards' chairs and silver crowns and an Oxford group and a revolving bookcase. We had a good walk over the fields and on dark lanes over the Lougher at nightfall. We spent the evening at Gwynfryn with George Williams now busy as headmaster of the new Secondary School there. Gwili has fewer pupils than ever and wants a better place, but meantime wears good black and smokes ad lib. I slept well. He wanted me to come back tonight and spend Sunday with him but I was pledged to spend it with Deacon if fine in an excursion to Ystradfellte. So I left at 9.30. By the way he was talking about modern Welsh plays and saying they all have poachers in them.

It was a lively warm bright morning with white clouds. The blackberries were thick but watery of taste, and bright in the yellow hedges mixed with dark alders and with grey fluffy bunches of hemp agrimony seeds as I went up to Carreg Cenen by Glyn Hir. Nobody was about as I went up and down between the rocky ferny hills and down into the valleys with white farms and walls and always ash trees. Ash trees by the waterfalls at Glyn Hir. A beautiful big one with very great upright limbs by the chapel called Bethany at Amanford: more up in the road up to Carreg Cenen and by the bridge at Pont Trapp and by the chapel and the pistyll that pours into the tarn where you turn to the castle: and one above the chapel on the hill with pale foliage in full sunlight but the ivy on its trunk very dark. The sun was pulsating in and out of passing clouds which came up over the long cairned ridge of the Black Mountains and the Beacons where Llynyfan lies under a wedge that was always darkest of all. The castle was always standing out with chimney-like fragments jutting up. I sat down at the highest point near Ferdre and smoked and looked N.E. towards Llynyfan.

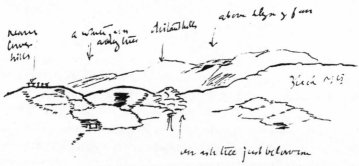

The dark outlines are the near hills through which my road was descending over little streams. The Black Mountains were on my right: on my side of them runs the Cenen under the copse of the lower slopes. The great hills were either stubble coloured and hedgeless or shadowed as with birch forests by the clouds, but none so dark as the wedge above Llynyfan. And beyond the Black Mts. once, I heard the boom of the blasting quarries. The road was all up for laying of pipes for the water from Llynyfan, English and Welsh navvies. I was first delayed by going back for my hat which I left when I was sitting. However by returning I made certain that a bird I had been hearing was the woodlark. It is a wild gentle timid song, not like a lark's so that you do not look for it up high but on trees or ground. But if you look up you see him 100 yards up making little flights and circling and hovering as if he lived there and never came down, not like the lark which soars up as high as he can get adventurously but really belongs to the earth. He stayed as long as I listened, singing all the time but with short intervals. The song is very sweet, wild and yet homely, something like a pipit's, but with a slight yodel and a smack of curlew too. As I sat there were several singing.

I was making for Gwynfe to circumvent the Black Mts. and return by Brynamman. The road was narrow and steep with high hedges of oak and hazel and alders and copses, and I got astray onto a *mountain* road, a rather rough one but shorter. However I had to turn back among some horned sheep by a brook because I was hungry. It was nearing 1. At Gwynfe – after passing several scattered cottages and a new 'Capel Maen' – I came to the little deserted plain towerless church and the bigger new one and the little grey Mason's Arms and had some bacon from a fat dirty but not illnatured woman and drank some good beer. She told me 4 navvies had stolen a ham lately – not a Welsh ham: you couldn't get one for love or less than a $1/4$ a pound. But she gave me Welsh bacon while she talked about an old dangerous lamp she was to let an English navvy have who was setting up housekeeping with some others and going to get a dog that would bite to look after it. I had no time to stay. I had 25 mountain miles to do in 3 hours. The first 3 or 4, after passing the Griffin and Newtown, the last cottage. I had to walk; it was a grand road hedgeless winding up over the bare stony hill with quarries and also loose heaps of stone high up almost like coal heaps by a railway station. At the narrow streams the road twisted sharply. The bridges were well above the stony shallow water and the mountain ash berries. Elsewhere there were no trees or bushes or even bracken, only ponies and stones and jackdaws and grass and some brooklime beside the road. Behind me were lower hedged hills and the high bare hills of the Towy and the Llyn-y-fan range beyond. Ahead the road could be seen nicking the skyline, and I imagined it was the highest point, but had many a turn before I came round by a quarry and a round stone limekiln and began the long descent to Brynamman's steep long street of dirty white houses, dogs lying in the road, and women and children talking to men in carts. I had been 1700 feet up. But had to be careful in descending because the road was bad and twisted and the fall on the left to the rather stony Garw was precipitous. Then I had an easy road mostly well above a streamlet in a decided valley with fern and oakwood on its slopes (Cwm Gors) – the Upper Clydach was the stream.

In another 6 or 7 miles I descended steeply into Pontardawe where roads cross a railway and a canal, and the Tawe river came through. The town is steel bar and tinplate works low down, but the hills make a ring where you can hardly see the gaps. Their bottoms are houses and works, their upper slopes wooded or dark with perpendicular quarries. It is a magnificent situation. Still the road was easy. I had a drink of water at a fountain (at Clydach) which says you will thirst again after it, and got on through Morriston always by tramlines beside a canal and Landore, coming in to Swansea, just at 4.30, that is in less than 3 hours and ate cockles and tart shortly afterwards.

Now the Williams' are out. I am not too tired, though my spine pricked me sometime before the end. It was always warm, even hot, and never seriously threatened to rain.

I found a letter from Mother here, but none from Frost.[3] So I wonder shall I go to Ryton. Father *is* retiring. He is at present away with my Uncle Evan near Newport.

On Wednesday night they were recalling Mrs Williams' mother saying in Welsh: 'Dai (David) helping Dick to do nothing.' 'That suits he as well as a watch does a toad.'

When she doubted a person, and knew something about him which she wouldn't mention, she said: 'Perhaps, indeed', only that.

John Williams remembers the chestnuts being planted which are now good trees at the edge of the road passing the big Hill House (or The Dales) in the steep cleft we passed going from Sketty to Cockett, where the magistrate lived of whom I spoke, one Coke (?) Fowler, said to be Warde Fowler's father.

The acorns were pretty, falling all the way along the lanes past Carreg Cenen, about as big as chaffinches eggs, pale soft apple yellow when they had just left the tree.

Later. A letter from Mrs Frost. They expect me on Wednesday. So address letters here up to *Monday first post.* I shall leave here early on Tuesday; probably stay Tuesday night at Brecon and reach the Frosts on Wednesday evening unless it's wet, in which case I shall train there on Tuesday, so please send Monday's, Tuesday's, Wednesday's and Thursday's letters to me at the Frosts'. I shall leave there on Friday or Saturday; perhaps I had better say Saturday. Then I shall arrive on Sunday, late afternoon most likely. I don't know where I shall stop on Saturday night.

A rum sight I forgot to mention near Cockett was a Gypsy caravan in the evening drawn on a waste bit with a hoop tent beside it and some clothes hanging out. Some of the children were searching for bits of coal in the refuse of a deserted colliery which was piled in their pitch. There was a gramophone going in the caravan. I could not see any name on their cart.

A new name for a pub I saw yesterday as I came down into Pontardawe, I think – Pheasant Bush.

I am so glad Baba recognized Blunderbore! I wish I could draw a sheep with long curled horns for her but I have tried and can't. I tried in vain to get her a photograph of Carreg Cenen, but I don't despair of finding her a castle.

79

I hope this is not too long. It's now Saturday morning and I will post in hope of reaching you tomorrow.

Baynes[4] wants me to go to Wisbech but I don't.

Goodbye all three. Edwy

I posted a letter yesterday from Amanford.

This is now the 5th. isn't it?

NLW

1 J.J. Williams, often called 'The Deacon', was headmaster at Waun Wen, Swansea
2 ET's cousins, who lived at Pontardulais.
3 ET met Robert Frost for the first time in November 1913. After a week at Easter 1914 spent together near Ledbury, their friendship ripened and was so fruitful during long discursive walks in August 1914 that ET subsequently said that Frost was 'the onlie begetter' of his own poetry.
4 Godwin Baynes, a fashionable doctor, friend of the Farjeons and of Bax. He hoped to cure ET of his depression.

32: *To Helen*

Thursday 24 February 1916   *Hare Hall, Gidea Park, Romford*[1]

Dearest

Fancy you thinking those verses had anything to do with you.[2] Fancy your thinking, too, that I should let you see them if they were. They are not to a woman at all. You know precisely all that I know of any woman I have cared a little for. They are as a matter of fact to father. So now, unless you choose to think I am deceiving you (which I don't think I ever did), you can be at ease again.

Silly old thing to jump so to conclusions. You might as well have concluded the verses to Mother were for you.[3] As to the other verses about love you know my usual belief is that I don't and can't love and haven't done for something near 20 years. You know too that you don't think my nature really compatible with love, being so clear and critical. You know how unlike I am to you, and you know that you love, so how can I? That is if you count love as any one feeling and not something varying infinitely with the variety of people.

Thank Bronwen for her letter and give her a large kiss.

We are all fairly deep in snow today. I got one snowball in the ear but luckily only on the flesh of the ear. There was a lot of snowballing. But we were indoors all day conducting an exam, which is very tiring. Tomorrow we don't know what we shall do. We have done with one lot; it will be a bad day to begin with another.

Goodbye now. I saw Father and Mother for an hour or so. I tried my tunic on, but I could get no change out of the compass man. I was back here again at 8.30.

I am all yours Edwy

---

1 ET enlisted in the Artists' Rifles in July 1915, and was sent to Hare Hall Camp as a map-reading instructor.
2 He refers to 'The Thrush': 'When Winter's ahead…'.
3 He refers to 'Nothing' [M.E.T.]: 'No one so much as you…'.

33: *To Helen*

1 March 1917   *Arras [Group H.Q.]*

Dearest

This afternoon I had nothing in particular to do and Berrington,[1] the Signals Officer of the Group, asked me to go along with him just to see how his telephone wires were being laid alongside the marsh at the edge of the city to our batteries (including 244). So I got the colonel to give me a little job to do on the way and we went out. It was sunny and warm with a fresh wind. I did what I had to do and while I was doing it Berrington sat down on the bank and smoked, which made him more or less forget what he had meant to do. Then we strolled on till a German plane came over and the alarm was blown and we sat down and smoked while the Anti-Aircraft sent scores of shells singing past us and spotted the plane with white puffs. The German had been going quite low over the city, taking photographs no doubt, but he rose up till he was as small as a lark and wasn't touched. Then another came over, apparently to direct the German artillery fire, for suddenly a shell came across and burst on the main road and 250 yards from 244. 244 were just firing their first rounds from their own guns. In a few seconds another shell burst in the same place, and that was the last of it for some reason or another. Berrington went along his wires almost as far as 244 and then we turned back and followed the wires towards the Exchange. This led us over the rising ground in front of 244 which we have been over quite freely of late. But the day was very clear and we could see the German lines and the ghastly village of ruined houses and dead trees that was my first sight of the enemy country a fortnight ago. At first I couldn't believe it, it looked so near. Yet the line of dead tall straight trees against the sky was quite unmistakeable. So as we were only 280 yards off we thought it best to sit down. We sat quite a little time and talked and smoked and looked through the glasses and watched yet another plane being peppered. A bullet of some sort fell some way off and made Berrington shut up his white map lest it was betraying us. Soon afterwards, and feeling a little chilled, we walked back and talked about architecture *a propos* the handsome great stables and riding school that we passed by, and the ruined cathedral that stood in front of the beautiful enormous 18th. century citadel on one side with a móat. He is a bit sharp and efficient and Fabian but we got on. He remembers Tilden slightly (he is an architect) by the way.

I doubt if we shall stroll into that ghastly village in a hurry. The enemy planes in these fine days spied out what has been done in the misty days and he will probably make it hot for us if we don't hurry up.

Now it is 5.50 p.m. Everybody is out except the Colonel who has another Colonel with him in the office, so I am alone in the dusk, and now this moment they have closed the shutters so that it seems night. It seems I am not escaping at once as the Colonel is having some difficulty in getting hold of the man who was to succeed me.

I have had a lot of Mother's cake and a lot of tea and my ears are burning. I should like to talk to someone as I can't write.

2 March. 6.30 a.m.

We are still being bombarded. But the Colonel and I have to go out to a village to see a man about a dog, you know, so I am having breakfast. I dressed soon after 5 because I thought it would be better if anything happened, to have my clothes on, and lying in bed warm one merely wondered which way It would come, whether through the ceiling or through which window or wall. Nothing fell on the house, though fragments were whistling over all the time and the house shook. However I heard men whistling in the street. Also when I got up and decided I would change my shirt etc. and shave and clean my teeth and eat my apple and drink my glass of water etc., these things sent the time along. The whistling outside of course made me certain the attack wasn't with gas shell. It is still going on, but more intermittently. At present it is very misty and I can see nothing but the garden tree and the stone dog on the wall.

I've been to — and back. From what the others say I gather that the bombardment was not so bad, as a lot of the noise was From us and not To us. I am new, you see. Well anyhow I was not upset.

It was quite nice to be going out in the misty frosty morning and picking a place to put a gun in a hurry.

Now I must try to see 244 today and get a letter from you which is probably waiting.

It is now 11 and I am having a second breakfast – (the first having been at 6.15) of marvellous good thick hard shortbread that Berrington has had sent him.

I hope you are all well, all of you, and enjoying many things. This goes off on March 2.

All and always yours Edwy

NLW

---

1 ET embarked for France on 29 January 1917. At 244 Siege Battery, ET's fellow officers were Major Lushington, Captain Horton, three young subalterns – Berrington, Smith and Rubin – and the older J.M. Thorburn, later my colleague at University College, Cardiff.

34: *To Helen*

Dearest

This has been quite a good day at the O.P. [Observation Post] and after a bad night of heavy shelling. The morning was bright and clear and all day long the sun shone and the sky has been pale and without a cloud. I have been drawing little panoramas. Those I had done last time are more interesting now because the Old Hun has been destroying many of the buildings on the skyline. Tonight he is burning something away in that direction. The sky is lit up with two big glows beyond the crest. It hasn't been tedious at all, and now we are installed in our dug out which hardly anything could penetrate. It is so small that if one moves the other five have to.

I am wondering if a letter has come for me at last. I think in any case I will keep this till I do hear, though Bronwen's letter implied that there was nothing abnormal.

To cram this little room still more the men insisted on dragging in one of the box spring mattresses from the other place. They had to cut it to fit it in at all, and now three of us are sitting on it; we have a door up, a fire going, one candle alight and can only hear the rustle of a Daily Mail.

Now it is 11 p.m. I have to be awake till 12. Then I sleep until 6 unless I am wanted which I shall be unless the night is quite quiet. So far there has only been a distant roll now and then as I sat reading 'Julius Ceasar', warm in front because of the fire, cold behind because of a door leading up into the street.

I dreamt (almost for the first time since I left home) last night – a very feeble dream, that I was at home but did not stay to tea. I don't know who was there. I was a sort of visitor and I could not stay to tea. I think Baba asked if I wouldn't stay to tea.

Every hour the telephonist tests the line to see if it is O.K. He has just done it and there is another hour to go before I begin to lie on those very bouncy springs.

Smith had a gramophone sent out to him. It arrived yesterday while he was at the O.P. So Rubin opened it and played him two tunes through the telephone. They still have Fortnum and Mason parcels every week. Horton has begun, too. But we are without flour, so that I am hard put to it to invent sweets. I invent all sorts of croquettes of rice and prunes or figs or marmalade fried in fat. I think them very good, but only Thorburn agrees with me. So they go in for tinned fruit – $3^1/_2$ francs for 10 half-pears!

Now I am back (Sunday the 18th) from the O.P., dirty and tired, but not much likely to have much rest as Thorburn and Smith have been taken away temporarily. But here's your letter and Eleanor's parcel. Alas! the letter you wrote at Hatch never came. So I have lost at least one in this blank week.

Well, it has been a pleasant 24 hours. One of the pretty things was to drive over an old green track running straight across No Man's Land and of course ending altogether in the trenches. Another pretty thing is the blue silent clear water of parts of the citadel moat, fed from chalk streams, but full of skeletons of small trees – some parts of the moat are osier and 'palm' (sallow) and there the water is stagnant and muddy. You walk alongside under enormous old ramparts of earth faced with stone and brick. There are trees, 70 or 80 years old, growing in the moat and just reaching the top. Well, what if there are? My dearest, if it weren't for these things I shouldn't be really alive. Actually now I hear a lark singing above the street as well as slops splashing out. And you must not convince yourself you are merely waiting, you know. You must have often been content or happy at Ivy's[1] if you can think of it, and however well life goes in war or peace, one doesn't get more than that, when you come to think of it, though of course I know you want more, and so do I.

I do hope Bronwen's finger is better. She wrote me a lovely letter in spite of it. My heart beats so fast at times, I wonder if it is oversmoking?

Now I am sure you are going to be happy with Baba in this lovely weather. I wonder when Easter is. I thought of Easter when yesterday was so warm. Today is Sunday when the Hun gets his ammunition and spends it too. What I said about planes is common knowledge over here. The result is we are almost powerless. The hope is that the best men have been resting during the winter. That is one theory.

Goodbye. Harry's idiotic remarks were about leave; where as I told you there is no leave at all in this Army except sick leave. I don't want leave. I would rather stay out till they don't want me any more. I couldn't bear to come home and return here. Goodbye. I hope all goes well.

All and always yours Edwy

NLW

1   Ivy Ransome, first wife of Arthur Ransome.

35: *To Helen*

Dearest

I was in that ghastly village today. The Major and I went up at 7.30 to observe; through the village was the quickest way. I never thought it would be so bad. It is nothing but dunes of piled up brick and stone with here and there a jagged piece of wall, except that the little summerhouse place under the trees that I told Baba about is more or less perfect. The only place one could recognize was the churchyard. Scores of tombstones were quite undamaged. All the trees were splintered and snapped and dead until you got to the outskirts. The trench we observed from ran along inside a garden hedge with a cherry in it. No Man's Land below the village was simply churned up dead filthy ground with tangled rusty barbed wire over it. The roads running through it had been very little damaged: one the actual trench cut through it. But the trees alongside were torn and broken and stripped. It was funny to come along a road and find that bit of ruin of a burnt house that I expected to have to observe from when we first came here. Then you wound round to it by deep trenches. They had begun to strengthen it for an O.P. and given it a fancy name. The well alone survives that is useful. – As the telephone was wrong we could not do a shoot from the O.P. so we came down again and went to our new position. On the way we saw a Bosh fight two of our planes. He set one on fire and chased the other off. The one on fire had a great red tail of flame, yet the pilot kept it under control for a minute or more till I suppose he was on fire and then suddenly it reeled and dropped in a string of tawdry fragments.

Our new position – fancy – was an old chalk pit in which a young copse of birch, hazel etc. has established itself. Our dugout is already here, dug by the battery we are evicting. It is almost a beautiful spot still and I am sitting warm in the sun on a heap of chalk with my back to the wall of the pit which is large and shallow. Fancy, an old chalk pit with moss and even a rabbit left in spite of the paths trodden almost all over it. It is beautiful and sunny and warm though cold in the shade. The chalk is dazzling.

The sallow catkins are soft dark white. All I have to do is to see that the men prepare the gun platforms in the right way, and put two men on to digging a latrine. – I am always devilish particular about that.

There are a few long large white clouds mostly low in the sky and several sausage balloons up and still some of our planes peppered all round with black Bosh smoke bursts.

I ate some oatcakes for lunch just now. They were delicious, hard and sweet.

The writing pads were quite all right, though no longer so necessary after Oscar had sent me half a dozen of these refills, which by the way are not very convenient except for short notes.

So you have found the village. We are not quite so far out as that, but between two villages and a little to this side. Both these villages are still shelled, but this particular place has never been shelled yet, so though I hear a big shell every now and then flop 200 or 300 yards away it feels entirely peaceful. But I can't get over the fact that there is no thrush singing in it. There is only a robin. I don't hear thrush ever. All the bright pale or ruddy stems in the copse and the moss underneath and the chalk showing through reminds me of Hampshire. The stone that the village whose name you know is built of is just like the Berryfield Cottage stone.

I heard from Sergeant Pearce[1] yesterday. There is no mapping in the battalion at all now, so he is working in the office where they deal with plans and billetings etc. for the Artists. He doesn't seem to mind it. He says he drives over with his wife to the village we used to walk to. Robin's sight had got worse (he injured his eye about a year ago) and he has apparently been discharged. I wonder what became of Mason. I keep forgetting or neglecting to write to Vernon. As to Benson, I forget the number of his battalion.

The wheat is very green in some of the fields a little behind us and they are ploughing near our orchard. I hope the old woman will get back to her cottage and apple trees and currant bushes and snowdrops and aconites and live happily ever after.

It is very idle of me to sit here writing, but the men are all at work and I can't help them except by appearing at intervals and suggesting something obvious that ought to be done. They will like the new position. It is full of dug-outs as it might have been of rabbit holes, a perfect little village of dug-outs, scattered about the copse alongside and in front of the guns. The copse is very little pulled about either. It is much like one of those chalk pits in Lupton's field only much larger. I shall soon go back to tea.

Now I have had tea and oatcakes and honey and also a cake from Burzard's Mrs Freeman sent me. I am having an agreeably idle evening, but then I am up with the lark tomorrow for 24 hours at the O.P. No letters today and tomorrow I shan't get them if there are any. Never mind. All is well.

I am all and always yours Edwy

The latest is that perhaps we shan't go into the chalk pit. The general is always changing his mind.

NLW

1   The names in this paragraph are of NCOs who were with ET in the Artists' Rifles.

36: *To Helen*

Dearest

Now the night is over I will tell you all about it before I go to bed, if I do go! I feel so cheerful for several reasons of which I will give you two. Firstly, I found a letter from you waiting for me when I returned at 7 a.m. Secondly, I found a car waiting for me as soon as I was clear of B [Beaurains], which was most cheering to a tired and overladen officer and four telephonists still more overladen. Well I didn't have much of the fire. I just waited to hear that the working party was only going to carry up the stuff, which they did, and to do the work today or some other time soon. I had to decide to let them carry the heavy stuff (too heavy for them to carry through a sticky trench) along the crest which was being swept by machine guns from time to time. Which they did and luckily came to no harm. I went off to the cellar, leaving two telephonists to take their instrument off the wire and see that the wire on to the cellar was all right. The cellar was full of smoke, except the lowest two feet of it, so that we (the two other telephonists and I) had to crouch or lie. Then shells began to fall in the direction of the O.P. In two hours the other telephonists had not arrived. I thought they had lost their way in the moonlight among the wire and ruins and trenches of B. or had been wounded – or perhaps the working party had had a casualty. So I sent back the other two telephonists to see if they had left the O.P. I had thought myself rather clever – or rather I was very much relieved – to find my way in the moonlight. There was also the complication that I had now been two hours away from the telephone, whereas I am always bound to be on hand. In about an hour the two returned to say the delay was caused by the shelling which had broken down the trench leading to the cellar and that they could not find the wire and that therefore two were staying on at the O.P. with the instrument. I ought to have gone back at once. Instead of which I dozed for one hour or two, dreaming of being court-martialled, till up I got and had a quiet journey. The moon had gone and left all the stars and not a cloud. I was sure of my way by the Plough. But it was dirty and tiring, for I had on

vest shirt two waistcoats tunic one Tommy's leather waistcoat British warm and waterproof.

Only two or three shells came over and I found the telephonists dozing and there in a clay corner we dozed and smoked till daybreak. More heavy shells arrived well away from us. They moan and then savagely stop moaning as they strike the ground with a flap. They are 5.9s or Five Nines as we call them. – I had not been wanted on the telephone so all is well. Day broke clear and white and a lark rose at 5.15. Blackbirds began to sing at 6 and a yellowhammer. I got up and slopped through the trench and looked at the view over to the Hun, a perfect simple view of three ridges, with a village and line of trees on the first, a clump on the second and clumps and lines on the furthest, all looking almost purple and brown like heather in the dawn. Easter Sunday – a lovely clear high dawn. Then I returned and sat and ate chocolate till the relieving party arrived at 6.30. I had a talk with the officer about the dugout and then off, so glad to be relieved and down through the ghastly street with a mule cart in it waiting for a shell to come over, and at the bottom the other two telephonists from the cellar. Half a mile further on past No Man's Land and that jagged ruin that I expected to observe from, with a well by it, known as the Burnt House, which now has the first five crosses of a Military Cemetery by it, I saw the motor car and we all joyrode back here. I washed, shaved and had a slow breakfast after reading your letter. At breakfast I read one from Ivy, such an artificial one, full of description, as if she thought that was what I should like.

Now everybody has breakfasted. There has been a shower and the sun has returned but among the clouds. I am not very sleepy yet, but just enjoying having nothing to do which is supposed to be the privilege of the day after the O.P. – that is in these peaceful days. You are having a fine Easter, I hope, as we are, though not a warm one yet. I like hearing of your days with Baba and Bronwen and Joy,[1] and of Mervyn's ride with Ernest, and intended ride to Jesse's. But here is Rubin saying he gets bored stiff if he is alone. Never mind. I liked hearing about your bath too and your working and the children eating. Rubin has set the gramophone to 'In Cellar Cool'. But everything, gramophone or not, out here forbids memories such as you have been writing. Memories I have but they are mixed up with my thoughts and feelings in B. or when I hear the blackbirds or when the old dog bangs the table leg with his tail or lies with his brains wasting in his skull. You must not therefore expect me to say anything outright. It is not my way, is it?

Now I must write and remind Mother she has sent only the inessential part of my mapcase, the waterproof cover for it.

A happy Easter! Goodbye
Edwy

NLW

---

1   The daughter of John Freeman.

37: *To Helen*

5 April 1917

Dearest

This is the second day, a much better day so far, beginning misty and turning warm. We have been firing faster, but I have sat in the sun at my job most of the time and got warm. I slept pretty well in the dug-out till our guns began. The other firing all night merely flapped and flapped like great sails in the heavy misty air. I woke hearing a wren sing and many blackbirds. The clods on my little hole where I work between 3 and 4 guns are getting fledged with fine green yarrow shoots all feathery.

The old dog this morning was delighted with running after Horton's stick and bringing it back. He laid it down and started gnawing it, and then barked for it to be thrown again. His barking delighted us very much. I don't think I had heard a dog bark in play for these three months. Then he went down into a shell-hole and drank the water in it.

The Somme pictures are absurd, compared with what I could tell you in five or six minutes and shall do someday I hope. Goodbye. I am all and always yours Edwy.

If there is a letter today I shall write more.

6 April 1917

There wasn't a letter… but I will add a little more. – The pace is slackening today.

Still not a thrush – but many blackbirds.

My dear, you must not ask me to say much more. I know that you must say much more because you feel much. But I, you see, must not feel anything. I am just as it were tunnelling underground and something sensible in my subconsciousness directs me not to think of the sun. At the end of the tunnel there is the sun. Honestly this is not the result of thinking; it is just an explanation of my state of mind which is really so entirely preoccupied with getting on through the tunnel that you might say I had forgotten there was a sun at either end, before or after this business. This will perhaps induce you to call me inhuman like the newspapers, just because for a time I have had my ears stopped – mind you I have not done it myself – to all but distant echoes of home and friends and England. If I could respond as you would like me to to your feelings I should be unable to go on with this job in ignorance whether it is to last weeks or months or years – I never even think whether it will be weeks or months or years. I don't even wonder if the drawers in the sitting room are kept locked!

Well, I can't get my hair cut this morning, so I shall go over to the battery soon and take a turn for Rubin or Thorburn. Smith is up at the O.P. today.

We have such fine moonlight nights now, pale hazy moonlight. Yesterday too we had a coloured sunset lingering in the sky and after that at intervals a bright brassy glare where they were burning waste cartridges. The sky of course winks with broad flashes almost all round at night and the air sags and flaps all night.

I expect there will be a letter today. Never think I can do without one any more than you can dearest. Kiss the children for me.

All and always yours
Edwy

NLW

38: *To Helen*

Dearest

Here I am in my valise on the floor of my dugout writing before sleeping. The artillery is like a stormy tide breaking on the shores of the full moon that rides high and clear among white cirrus clouds. It has been a day of cold feet in the O.P. I had to go unexpectedly. When I posted my letter and Civil Liabilities paper in the morning I thought it would be a bad day, but we did all the shelling. Hardly anything came near the O.P. or even the village. I simply watched the shells changing the landscape. The pretty village among trees that I first saw two weeks ago is now just ruins among violated stark tree trunks. But the sun shone and larks and partridge and magpies and hedgesparrows made love and the trench was being made passable for the wounded that will be harvested in a day or two. Either the Bosh is beaten or he is going to surprise us. The air was full of aeroplane fights. I saw one enemy fall on fire and one of ours tumble into the enemy's wire. I am tired but resting.

Yesterday afternoon was more exciting. Our billet was shelled. The shell fell all round and you should have seen Horton and me dodging them. It was quite fun for me, though he was genuinely alarmed, being more experienced. None of us was injured and our house escaped. Then we went off in the car in the rain to buy things.

We shall be enormously busy now. Rubin goes off tomorrow on a course of instruction and may be a captain before long; our sergeant major has left with a commission. One officer has to be at the O.P. every day and every other night. So it will be all work now till further notice – days of ten times the ordinary work too. So goodnight and I hope you sleep no worse than I do.

Sunday. I slept jolly well and now it is sunshine and wind and we are in for a long day and I must post this when I can.

All and always yours Edwy

NLW

39: *To Edward*[1]

My darling my own soul. I know that this pain will go and calm and even happiness come again, just as this snow will melt, and let the Spring come, for in the earth is life moving all the time, and in our souls love is eternal. And that's all that matters. All that matters is that we love each other and that sooner or later we shall understand as we cannot understand now.

Farewell sweetheart, and believe that when courage comes back to me as it will you will not find me wanting. This snow must be the last of this terrible winter, that will help me, but more than all your trust in me.

Farewell and God bless you and keep you and bring you back to me whose heart and soul and body are yours ever and wholly,
Helen
Baba says 'give Daddy 100 loves'.

ETC

---

1 Helen's last letter to Edward, strangely creased and stained, was returned to her after his death. None of her daily letters to him in France have survived.

A Postscript

April 9th to June 17th [1917]

Beloved, there have been many weeks and now I have come to today. The way has been very difficult for me, but even through darkness and despair and just nothingness and fear, just as ever when these things came before, all has been well at last because of our love.

I saw the Spring come sweet heart. Such a Spring of flowers and birds and colour and peace and sound after all that terrible winter. All the flowers came out together, except the May which was very late. We found it once on May Day do you remember! And lying in the orchard under very old apple trees heavy with blossom and full of bees I listened to the nightingale and the cuckoo and touched the moist green grass and lay listening and looking and hearing and touching and filling my soul with it and gather it all into myself as I have gathered you in my arms beloved. Because it is you I feel in it all, and we are very close all the time and I am almost content sweet heart that it should be so.

For myself sweet and for you I am content. I said often to you I could wait and wait contentedly if only I knew that we should be together again and so I can wait doing all you have left me to do.

For the children – this is my fear. I am so unstable. You went through life seeking the truth and always on a chosen and straight path, straight ahead without doubt. But I cannot do that. I did not really know what is true and what untrue. I am persuaded and deceived and yet I think I shall not go far wrong with your dear hand in mine. I shall take that letter you wrote to Merfyn as my text: 'Be honest and kind', and teach that to the children.

Now after much wandering and restlessness I am back at the cottage and for a while alone, but wonderfully at ease. This perfect midsummer day, the heat, the roses everywhere gives me such strength such hope, because the more beautiful things are the more I feel you near to me my beloved, my precious one.

Do you feel, do you know what love you left in the hearts of your friends, what love you made in the hearts of the men with whom you worked. Oh sweet heart how proud I am. Such love very few men inspire; it was your truth I think and your beauty, your beautiful face, your voice, your soul looking out of those grey eyes. How I love you dear heart. I thought my heart would break, but my love held it fast.

Bronwen is away at Dorothy's[1] having such a lovely time, among cowslips and pigs and dogs and the country things we love her to be among. Baba is at Annerly, happy too with the children, but I want her home.

The war is into a state, a little nearer the end sweet heart because of all you did, but terror and death and grief are still around us, like a hideous dream it has become. Yet out of it what beauty has been! I think more than all the cruelty the pain the ugliness of it, the beauty and strength and courage and sacrifice that has come of it will love and shine and make for good. That is why you died beloved.

Now I must get to my work. Never away from you, never even unconscious of your nearness and all my dependence on you. I take in my hand your great bent thumb as I used to do. For a little while, Farewell.

From Helen's Commonplace Book *in the Edward Thomas Collection.*

1 Bronwen was with Mrs Locke Ellis, Myfanwy at John Freeman's.

Appendix

Seven Letters to Harry and Janet Hooton

Janet Hooton (*née* Aldis) remained Helen's lifelong friend from their schooldays. The Hootons witnessed the marriage of Edward and Helen on 20 June 1899 at Fulham Registry Office and then agreed that Helen should stay with them at Gipsy Hill until her baby was born. Eventually, Edward gained consent for Helen to live with his parents until his Final Schools in June 1900. Harry Hooton shared Edward's love of long-distance walking and they met frequently for short stays until Edward's death. Edward's intermittent letters to Harry and Janet confirm that, apart from Edward's much later friendship with Robert Frost – and Helen's close ties with her sisters Irene and Mary – the close Hooton-Thomas relationship lasted as long as they lived. In his letters to Harry Edward opened up his thinking freely, especially in his early Oxford days, when he signed himself 'Edwy', his Welsh family name. Later on he sent Harry his first large group of poems, inviting his approval and comments. It is no surprise that Edward's private doubts about the outcome of the war appear in his final short letter to Janet Hooton, a few days before his death near Arras. This brief selection of Edward's letters to Harry and Janet seemed the most natural accompaniment to the familiar correspondence between Helen and Edward.

Unfortunately, none of Harry's letters to Edward survive. But all of Harry Hooton's books, notes and correspondence – including his 1949 memoir, *Edwy* – are in the Colbeck Collection at the University of British Colombia, Vancouver. I have deposited photocopies of numerous typescripts of ET's letters to HH in the *Edward Thomas Collection* at Cardiff, plus a selection of notes written by Harry at the end of most of Edward's texts. The letters here printed are based on the Vancouver originals which consist of 167 letters from Edward to Harry, 7 from Edward to Janet, and 3 from Helen to Harry and Janet after Edward's death. The letters to Harry are concentrated in two groups – 45 between 1897 and 1902, 105 between 1909 and 1917 – with a mere 26 between 1903 and 1908. In his memoir Harry states: 'There were long series of walks together, sometimes for long days, at others for 2 or 3 days at a time... our ritual was unvaried, we just walked in healing silence.'

I still find it difficult to read these early letters without a growing (*post-hoc?*) awareness that in them the prose-poet was already beginning to grope his way towards the daylight world of poetry. And this despite an early disclaimer to Harry: 'Some things I write in prose ought to be in verse, to have effect, but I am too old to begin such an arduous art, as I recognize it to be.' (24 November 1897). Here are two of many examples in ET's notebooks of moods engendered during the 'healing silences' of these walks with Harry:

30 Nov. 1902: Out in a gentle dawn without wind, and seemed to be one with the pool that dimpled, and the trees that dripped, and the grass that hummed, in my enjoyment of the rain. Perhaps some subtler being saw me moved by the silence and solitude, – as I saw the pool. Would that I could clothe my naked thoughts in the garment of a mood, and saw what manner of medicine for the soul the rain dispensed.

21. Nov. 1905: I saw all the oaks of the Big Meadow and of the horizon woods beyond suddenly and for 5 minutes glow so that they were simply animated colour – the colour of all the hues copper and gold ever attained and more (because of varieties of surface); the colour revealed against a very deep lustrous blue sky during the Gleam. There they were – all the oaks in the Big Meadow, the Big One in the hedge (which is laced with bright colours among the dark), and the mass at horizon – everything but colour forgotten – but that colour was joy and health and song. The song of colour.

Notebook 12 in particular, which covers many of their Pilgrims' Way walks together, sheds light on the significance of Edward's early submission of his poems to Harry for comment.[1] At the same time, too, Edward once more signed his letters to

Harry with the Welsh form Edwy which Edward had insisted that Harry should adopt in their early letters to each other. This close friendship lies beneath the poignancy of Harry's recall of their last one-day meeting at Epping Forest (High Beech, near Loughton):

I watched him, not without surprise, calmly and methodically, even cheerfully, going through the ordinary ritual of a social day, while I myself was full of foreboding. I realised something of the congregated horror of the nations watching their young depart in crowds on their ridiculous crusades, ridiculous, but with possibilities not to be thought of! And so we passed an outwardly cheerful day, warding off those thoughts that were not to be thought, until at last the happy day – the ordeal – drew to an end. Helen, like millions of other Helens all over the world, drawing a silent veil of decent heroism over these partings. Helen was cheerful to the last, and we resolutely said our last Au revoir.

This continuation of the healing silences that surrounded the numerous walks they had made together over nearly twenty years fructified the mutual trust of these closest of friends. It comes through Helen's letter of thanks to Harry when she received his *Edwy* memoir:

One aspect of it particularly delighted me that you bring out the fun and the social charm of Edward and not as I think is the great fault of John Moore's book dwell distortedly on the unhappiness and strain. We know there were these elements in great degree but they never clouded for ever the funloving, openair-loving, lovely friend of all sorts of men that Edward was. Another aspect that of course pleases me that you make me so nice, and show your love for me so sweetly. Thank you dear oldest (except Janet) friend.

Edward's letters clearly reveal how his daimon – the persistent need to comprehend his own nature – was a lifelong taskmaster. With his War Diary, they uncover his deepening acceptance of things as they are – the need to live to the moment and not for it. His poems are not an escape from the complexities of hard thought, as so many of his 'prose poems' were: at their roots, they draw upon a series of experiences scattered at random throughout his voluminous prose writings. But what is so happily in place in the poems is the acceptance of moments, in and out of time, that bring to everyday living a sense of exultation and self-forgetfulness. Thomas once wrote that 'a great writer so uses the words of everyday that they become a code of his own which the world is bound to learn and in the end take to itself'. The numerous early letters to Harry Hooton exhibit this process.

1   As far as I can discover, ET sent early copies of poems to a very select circle of friends: Harry, James Guthrie, Gordon Bottomley and then to De la Mare.

113, Cowley Road, Oxford

My dear Hooton,

It would feel like neglect and temperance not to do something, after reading this your letter; so, although I know I cannot finish this letter, and I think not probably for some days, and despite my partial weariness and occupation I will write a line, if only to say, that I can say nothing. Any return would be too small which was not instant: my feeling in response to your tenderness was instant: therefore, lest even friendship and kindness should forget or be deceived, I go the length of saying that I write but a moment after the reading of your letter. I do think that if someone I loved told me that he had acted so, I should rejoice. As I, though reluctantly conceding equality of feeling to anyone, such is my egoism, feel that you are here in the same case. I tell you how I touched deeply along your letter; hoping even such a little can content, if it cannot, as it should not, satisfy.

One more word tonight. Have you thus early enough sympathy to remind me in some way, if at any time my quite undoubted egoism goes too far from childishness to be amiable, or tolerable. This sounds like disingenuousness. But you will come to see that I can write, by no means only bulk and think, only by myself, with a most perverse analytic minuteness; so far, that perhaps you will frown and stamp in watching one at a microscope who never looked up, but talked and murmured as he worked; as I write, I feel myself looking and behaving very much like that. There is the great failing of letters. It is that which almost persuades me never to write anything beyond civil news; it is a weariness to fumble for truth and completeness, and after all to feel the failure at both. Living words alone could speak plain. Truly my living words could vindicate me; ask Helen, if they would not. Goodnight.

Rather than say much, and yet not all, and have the mortification of failing to reach an end and of awakening hopes which the conclusion does not satisfy, I would almost not write at all, or only greetings; for then the most uncharitable would give me credit for more, and the imagination of the uncharitable would work towards some beauty that was not in the letter, yet

I never found myself. You are charitable, I am so exacting. Once more, Goodnight.

No: I find, after waiting at my work a little time, that I cannot avoid finishing this letter. The thought haunts and troubles me so, the thought that I cannot satisfy you, or adequately express my real self even, which might not satisfy you in its entirety. After resolving that, I had nearly determined to ask you to excuse me from writing ever at length; but it was apparent, that would be a poor provision. I know I could endure silence from any friend at all very ill for so long a time: and with you it would be the same. Besides, I fear in such times, men cannot easily live on their thoughts and imaginations alone; not even lovers. So it would be vain if our friendship is to be anything, to attempt a silence. Then we must do our best – I must do my best, always hoping infinitely for the time when we can be much and long together.

I feel I might attempt a story of this place, and of the few among its people whom I have met, and of my life here. The country also might touch you. But absolutely I have not the time. I admit I have often used such an excuse when it was vain; now I find it actually true. Lectures of a useless kind for Responsions occupy three hours for six days a week; besides which I have all my much History for the Balliol Scholarship three weeks ahead; and more, my writing, that must have an hour or two each week, since more and more, I fancy, it becomes, solid and worthy, or less and less fickle and loose and poor. Here I can fancy your smiles, if you have seen my book.[1] But indeed my writing is far different now; utterly different in style and subject. If I did not fear to come to the test, I would send you a paper of mine 'Shadow of the Hills' which the *Speaker* prints shortly: it was once good enough, but I had to hack it and piece it to suit the paper.

I can not write much more: but one confession I ought to make, though I daresay it is a kind of involved conceit which causes me to make it; I am fearfully conceited: and yet, in palliation I say it, I am constantly and honestly deprecating that your knowledge of men will tell you it is a common case, it maybe: pray think kindly of it. And I am fearfully selfish, as in everyday matters, of little deeds and more. Is this compatible with a generosity of spirit such as I arrogate for myself? To speak low, but truthfully and to the point: I borrow money, but never lend: I do many little underhand things to satisfy my only physical craving – that for books and still more books.

There was something in my calling you Mister. I don't know that I ever called a man by his surname in my life; and if I didn't call him by his Christian name, I abstained. And many older men than myself I always call Mister in letters and speech, as when I was a little child. What may I call you then?

Though I may not write, do you write when you can! Let me not, after this one grace, have that feeling which I daily have in broken hopes, like that feeling of one who watches bright wine spilt into sand. Let me still hold to you: the very wish you have of pleasing me is enough, I assure you: nor do I look for help in the ways of life, so much as the senseless comforts our Mothers give us, only that... Because you cannot solve a difficulty for me is no reason why our friendship should not be perfect. I have no faith in affinities or contraries of nature in friendship; but faith only in what is alike in all, and knows not affinity or contrary; the trouble being to reach that place in another man. I believe you never can offend me or my sense; but I cannot believe I shall not offend you, knowing my faults, and failures to do what I speak. Love, give us love. and so I leave you with an infinite trust. On earth there is perhaps only one perfection, one beauty, that of the physical and spiritual union of two creatures, man and woman: for the highest that is beneath that, I have a hope in you. I know I am right I will bear no contradiction. But by no means do I know I am good or lovely. But I have faith. Yours, hoping all things and having much, yours, although I feel so often, as in my babyish verses (Lo, in the heart of Summer's bud, the worm!) I said I did.

Yours hopefully, Edward Thomas.

1   *The Woodland Life*, 1897

109

My dear Harry,

I am beginning to fancy and half believe all sorts of stupidities about your forgetting me, or even that you are not well, simply because you have not written this week. Indeed I have been chafing a little. 'Then why not write?' That is so true! And largely lest you should think I intended only to write after having a letter from you, I sat down just now, at the end of my long day. For I could not bear to feel that you had that opinion.

In fact, I have been busier than ever this week, I hope not too busy. The result of which is lamentable exceedingly; I have hardly given a thought to anybody, but only to things and shadowy things; my head has been full of Charles V, Louis XIV, Frederick the Great, and their many valets. So this cramming – it is of course not study – has quite banished humanity from me, or me from humanity, and I am in danger of becoming a mere dry stick, a thing I always have been near to, if I am to believe people.

Yes: it vexes me a good deal, to think of the waste of time this is. All my reading and all my thinking done at such a flurried pace as this will have to be undone, and re-read, re-thought. I glance at deeds and strengths, nobility and vice with a kind of sorrow that for such mercenary reasons I am compelled to pass them with only a glimpse. So many pages in so many hours, so many books in so many days; goodness, it ought soon to end. For which reason alone, I might wish for success, that would leave me to settle down into a calm labour. I begin to think I may have things to do in the world beside write prose fancies. Who can tell? I certainly can not tell, but am always trying to tell, with much waste of time and temper, and much of the ridiculous in the attempt. Nor is it possible to tell just now, perhaps. For even supposing I were ever capable of forming ideas and of carrying them through to truth, this were not the air to encourage my capability or to exhibit it. All I do is to try to be original, laughing at myself in my own sleeve, in the hope that I shall get the Scholarship. This may surprise and puzzle you. I will explain. Here at Oxford, they give History Scholarships essentially not for knowledge of facts but for what they call ideas, theories, and so on. Whereas, I know very well people of my age can't have ideas or theories; or ought not to, anyhow, according to reason and right. You see, it encourages fantasy, air-castle building, and 'the wild imagination essential to political economists'. Not that I am entrapped by this requirement of theirs; for I see its folly and direst wrongness; but that I am bound to obey it for success. And after all, it is a great issue for me; this Scholarship. – But let me drop it. It is unwise, profitless, unhealthy to talk of chance. Chance alone it is. I know I deserve a scholarship. Unhappily I by no means know I shall get one. I have no reason to hope I ever shall. Wrong, therefore, there is, if I speak truly, as you can perceive.

'A shadow of a magnitude!' Isn't that a glorious phrase? Keats wrote it, as you know, in his Sonnet on the Elgin Marbles. I long ago recollected it, to tantalise my memory for months; it was so grand I thought it Virgil's; for Virgil has a similar, 'Magni nominis umbra' – the shadow of a mighty name. And if you please, all I can do with it is, hope I may have an opportunity of calling the Holy Roman Empire 'a shadow of a magnitude'! Impudent fool that I am. All the same, I see the true worth, I hope, of this line. Keats has much of such, but all too little.

And so goodnight. There is a high blue moon tonight and many stars. Underneath, the world is yelling and sinning, and I am writing small talk. Ay me. But I know my smallness. 'Yet I know my words are wild.'

Sunday. I have just come in very silly and very cold, so I shall be, as you perceive, more illegible and unreadable than ever. It is a very pleasant country here; but the pleasanter the less endurable is country in unfortunate company; and mine was unfortunate. I ejaculated about six yeas and nos in the course of two hours. In consequence, I am put down as an idiot. But is one bound to talk of one's dinner etc.? Or if not, is one bound to interject some sage or saintly subject by way of change? I did neither. The only alleviating point in this walk was the number of pretty women and girls; so as I delight in looking at such, I very rudely looked into the eyes of those that passed. As to this, will you think my spirit the same as that of those who speak of 'pretty girls'? Surely not. And I never want really to go beyond looking at them, as probably, most of them would be sadly disappointing if they spoke, being of the 'lower' or 'lower middle' well-dressed class. It always has been so with me, and will be. Also, in my thought it is neither vulgar nor stupid. – I get an extraordinary pleasure thus. And let me explain what I meant by that silly passage in my last letter, about expensively dressed girls. It was this. My cousins are rather wealthy, and so wear rich dresses, which I am never tired of hearing – oh, those sounding silks, so uncomfortable, so gorgeous. Yes I like comfortable dresses, too: why not? All I don't like is rags, ill taste, ill-shapes. Here again I speak stupidly in spite of the real soundness of my thought. If only I could actually talk with you. I should explain, convince and delight you, so sanguine am I; and I am the more confident because my feeling for girls has still the same nervous reverence of childhood or earliest boyhood, rather increased if anything, and only too excessive to be chivalrous. In my childish days I remember I used to fear to touch the little girls sleeves; so it is now. If I retain any true innocence it is here. Otherwise to a great and unhappy extent I am like Rousseau when he left Italy at age of about 16. You remember in the Confessions? He says (I haven't the book here) 'I returned with my "virginity but not my maidenhead"' which is a bad but suggestive translation. So it must be now-a-days. This reminds me that I ought to say how I enjoyed reading Rousseau's Confessions, in the original and complete form of course, for my French is fairly good. There was nothing foul or revolting in it, unless it were the Parisian madames whom he met. As for his being a sensualist, a beast – how absurd to think so. He was some times indiscrete; his sentiment is often false; and he has no tact: but he is always ingenuous, straightforward, almost innocent. I retain many vivid memories of the whole book. I read it in May June and July this year. It was all so different to what foul Englishmen had led me to expect. John Morley's 'humid warmth', 'unhealthy hothouse humidity' as applied to Rousseau's love-making is partly correct, it is true, but too strong and unsympathetic. And I found it only too incomplete as a Confession; so much so that, if he says all true, he was a saint almost – except for poor Therese.

112

The misrepresentation of Rousseau recalls the misrepresentation of Sappho. Why is it women make so little of that glory of her sex? Is it because the vulgar call her by no delicate name, whore, light woman? I am afraid so. But I am drawn much to her poetry, and the more so, because the father of an acquaintance of mine here wrote a very complete book on her; his name is Henry Thornton Wharton. Sappho of course wrote mainly love and bridal poems, of which we have fragments alas too few. But one thing we have, her glorious epithet 'violet weaving'. She cries 'Violet-weaving Aphrodite!' Then do you recollect the verses of Tennyson's 'Rosalind', the best of his simpering Juvenalia?

'The ancient poetess singeth that Hesperus all things
    bringeth
Soothing the weary mind: bring me my sweet Rosalind.'

Is not that an exquisite imagination? that Hesperus brings all things to those who yearn. And Tennyson has elaborated it, as was too often his practice, in many poems. Greatest of women, Sappho! Mrs. Barrett Browning indeed! The difference is so clear. Tear Sappho's clothes from her, she is a woman, beautiful, passionate, almost glowing. Tear – God forbid! She is very virtuous, but so also is the late Editor of the *Chronicle*.

But this is too literary; neither so bad as a causerie, nor so unaffected as friendship perhaps you think. How I long for time, really to talk, not to gibber feverishly like this.

Pardon all my omissions and all my wrongdoing, won't you. It is just in that pardoning that love differs from liking. Love is not jealous. Fancy, Catullus loved Clodia. The incestuous glorious Clodia, the most beautiful in Rome; wealthy, powerful, and yet a foul slave to her body. And Catallus loved her, called her Lesbia! You will pardon me. I will try to write again soon.

Commend me to Janet, if I have not injured her by my trifling.
Edwy.

I send this to Lombard Street; because I could not clearly read your Earl's Court address.

My dear Harry

I am very much ashamed of my letters to you in some ways; and I must express this shame, although I hear you even now censuring me for my want of confidence; for this reason. The intellect does not much enter into friendship, and hardly at all into any I could form, I think. Yet it is of the intellectual portion I am ashamed: for certainly such a complete want of order, thought, and every sort of care and moderation, could not be exceeded. If it were only for the sake of giving you as little trouble as may be, I ought to have more attended to this. It is, however, not for you that I regret this giddy manner! It is because I ought, at my age, and with my reading and my pretentions above all, to have reached some sense of the arrangement and coolness which I should always aim at, to give my writing the utmost perspicuity attainable. This I think I have ludicrously failed to do. I have also failed in appearance to have even conceived that such consideration was necessary. All which is a great mistake; which must have unhappy result if I do not make some sort of change. The natural thing, therefore, is at once to attempt a change. Immediately I come to a standstill, with the grotesque interrogation, How change? Grotesque it is; nevertheless it is true that I don't know how to change. For, with all my fevered but perpetual self analysis, I know nothing of myself, and can not see, by the closest examination , what I am to apply myself to, in order to effect this change. Nay more; I do not know how to examine even! Here I think I realise that my words border on impossibility and the land of darkness, dreams and chimeras. Allowing for my limitations, it is probable that nobody ever did what I have just said I could not do. Possibly you have not been able to follow me: I have in fact come to a precipice as infinite as that where we stand in asking why we exists: have I not? – Then you have followed me.

This eminently grammatical – it is pretty fairly so – but empty talk leaves me where I began. I am ashamed that my letters appear only first impressions which I seem to fling at you in my heat and before I have carefully weighed them; often they may appear not my impressions, but only the spinnings of an unbalanced and scantily gifted brain: that is it: there I express myself exactly.

So I will, in my future letters, confine myself to relating experiences, announcing and explaining what events may interest both, recording with especial care and restraint my opinions of what I read and see and hear, and with still more care and restraint my imaginations, if I am so uncontrolled as after this to have any, and my thoughts, if after a pitiless censure I can decide that they are possible for me. May I be allowed one license? I shall never stop by nature to consider what I shall say about my feeling for you. That I know you will permit; supposing you have entertained anything but amused and kindly contempt for this lengthy affair, which itself is little more than an exaggerated but somewhat more prosaic process of the same old self criticism.

I need to give you some very large proof of my unaltered love, after this stilted enunciation: — I have not once halted in my affection, nor doubted yours, though you have been so long silent that in another it would have driven me to wordy despair or to hopeless resignation.

It strikes me that my style here is very stiff and awkward, even if it is correct; but do not therefore conclude I am heartlessly elaborating a formal essay; for the only cause I can think of is, that I have just been very carefully translating Caesar for the sake of my writing, which is a remedy I rather believe in. I can write very few more words this evening, for it grows late. But one thing I must say is, I should like to be able to write well and consistently; one of my regrets being that my time is too completely occupied for much practice; and that practice being, now at any rate, in letters alone, is itself hurried to uselessness. Clear-headedness, if not actual thinking power, is absolutely necessary for a good style. I am exquisitely wrong-headed. So I conceive that anything beyond a modest mediocrity is unattainable. That modesty is itself not inconsiderable as a merit, and may be cultivated at all times: for me, in particular, with my vast and gorgeous visions, it supplies a boundless prospect of labour in the attaining, by relentless processes of pruning and levelling.

And now goodnight: I am the same well meaning creature that

still cry over thin sentiment and bathos, and that give myself up entirely for the moment to whomsoever will smile on my passionate enthusiasm: even now I am thinking of coming winter nights under a high moon and the Pleiades with you. Goodnight.

My dear Harry

I sat down last night to begin a letter for you, and as it was a quite ingenuous one and a picture of myself I will send it also; but I can not let it stand at the opening because I now see how very unlike it is to what this latest letter of yours demands in answer. It would shock you to put your hand on beauty and then find it marble. It would shock me to prove marble to your touch. So I relegate its decorous good nature to the end; which I do the more especially as in this letter you do in so many words proclaim that you will not tolerate anything like an essay.

It delights me to think you could have wished for me to be with you at any critical time; it would have delighted me and satisfied me even if I could have been with you when you wished. I always have a keen consciousness of something in myself which is perpetually behind all my actions (as it were), waiting to be satisfied, but never satisfied. It is something altogether unconnected with the senses or the brain; as I fancy, it is something infinitely nobler and deeper than they can be. Moreover, there are cases in which it is very easy for me to imagine this satisfaction actually completed. On these cases I constantly dwell: and sometimes they are so far possible and not purely ethereal, that I have them in anticipation: but as yet except with one woman I have never been near to achieving it. Strange to say, it is a point of a very inferior kind, as we generally think, which has stood in my way. To tell the exact truth: a horrible contortion seems to come over my face, and a chill to run about my limbs at the critical moment when, bodily or spiritually as it may happen, I am about to throw myself upon the person who is the object of my passion: and most grotesquely this uncomfortable feeling is in kind the same as we experience in the company of fools who are foolish and vain people who are vain and yet they know it not; in fact a ghastly smile creeps on to my face as when I assent to the remarks of one whom I despise or

---

* A final note above the address: 'What a matter I have made of it: only now realizing my exuberance. Can you ever read it all. Good heavens, what a thing it is.'

dislike. In this I fancy I am singular , at least in its exaggeration. So many times have I built up hopes on a foundation which I afterwards acknowledge as nothing; I have, as I told you, a way of falling in love with all I meet, and a way also of being invariably disappointed.

I will tell you a little incident of a few days ago, though after it I felt I had been in a way disloyal to you or to my feeling for you. I frequently see a man here whom I knew and a little liked at St. Pauls.[1] I always thought him the most exquisitely gentle and sympathetic creature, but could never form any hope of being more than his well-treated acquaintance. His attitude towards me was curious, now I reflect on it: he used rather to flatter me in a way that at that time used to flatter a tremulous personal vanity of mine. Well, I met him at Trinity, his College, and several times lunched with him. But as one other person was always there it was for me absolutely impossible to come to a true understanding. Nevertheless he was constantly kind, and, although I must have annoyed him by my stupid silence, he continued to invite me. I invited him in return. During tea we spoke, being alone, pretty freely and rapidly about likings we found we had in common, for instance, religious pictures of Italians like Botticelli and Fra Angelico. Then we went out together, I talking most, he assenting, though he is three years older than I and of infinitely more experience. I described to him pictures which I cared for, pictures I am nearly enough of a mediaeval Catholic to worship. So we talked; my heart beating quickly and nearly choking me; the only hesitation I had coming in the form of that thrill, when I seemed to have been too passionate and frank. On the way we met a child crying. My acquaintance in his simple way took the child's hand and asked him what ailed him. At the same time I got down his cap which someone had hidden away, and put it on his head; I was too timorous to do more. We left the child comforted, and were all the closer for a common compassion; my acquaintance took my arm and was certainly as entirely rapt as I; but I continued to speak all the time, being so full of pent up feeling and thought about things and people in my long lonelinesses. He had to leave me shortly. He went: and it was one of my entirest pleasures to hear him, he who had so many friends and acquaintances, he who was so affectionate, so unembarrassed, so much in society, so entirely different to me, to hear him say that he liked me very much, smiling all the time in a truthful childish way. I saw him the next day (Wednesday), and that was different; nor have I seen him since. Thus it is, Harry, that my hopes expire. I have one sumptuous and voluptuous bridal: but, like Psyche, my bride opens her eyes; and I, like Eros, leave her weeping, but compelled to leave the distrustful one.

So I return to you: and now you can see with what joy I return from disappointment and momentary delights to you who can not disappoint me, who all along give me a placid delight, and will often in the future give me delights just as rich as those momentary ones. It is thus I felt when my blood cooled, my face unflushed, my heart paused, and I was myself again. Nor, even in my highest emotion, could I forget you, though my rapture was entire at the time.

Of course this is all by way of parenthesis.

Now, however, you say you having nothing much to torment you, yet still look forward to our meetings. So do I. I shall have about six weeks vacation, beginning about December 14, in which I hope I shall see you often, if I may. And I want you very much to see Helen, though the new change she is to make so shortly will separate us a little more than usual:[2] – there again, if I had any morality, I should melt with self reproach that she should suffer as she does and must for some time yet. What shall we do whenever we can be in company? Being such imperfect creatures, clogged by such weights of mere animal flesh and sense, we shall not be able to jump together immediately; through books I expect we shall approach one another – I have no idea what you read, but have no doubt we shall find a common point in the long roll of people whom I delight in: hardly a poet whom I don't like, even such incompatibles as Shelley and Arnold. I hate almost nobody in literature, though I avoid many who now write. I hate Walt Whitman as I hate prostitution, not prostitutes, and as I hate disease. No fouler insolence ever wrote:

Dabs of music

119

Dewy-orbed underlapped brothers
I turn the bridegroom out of bed and lie with
the bride myself: I tighten her &c.

He is an added fiend to Hell. I like and admire Byron; but this beastly democrat is too much for me.

However, you read, I think a good deal of what is written nowadays. I wish you would tell me of it; for it is one of my greatest offences that small as I am I affect to despise those of my own day. You mentioned John Davidson: now can you tell me something of him. I know and despise his prose, such as 'A Random Itinerary', and could not expect much from its author in any way, but should rejoice if you could convince me. Thomas Hardy I sympathise with, though I only know Tess. Then there is a whole crowd, Andrew Lang and more, who could do useful things if they confined themselves to the journey-man work of literature, but corrupt and degrade otherwise. They tell me Lang's style is good; and his Daily News leaders are smartly written, I own: but if you want to see his limits, read the translations of Theocritus and Homer, which have an absurd want of balance and moderation. I don't quarrel – an admission that is itself stupid – with the men, but rather with their admirers who have no conception of place and propriety; after that they themselves seem to fill with the conceit and the result is [Richard] Le Gallienne. Then there is Swinburne, who has written laudable hexameters, but what else. Ten years ago he said Shelley was the greatest and would always be the greatest lyric poet; now he thinks him empty and worthless. What can one make of such a man? Robert Louis Stevenson's style was pretty and graceful; but false, simply because it was thin: whereas no good style can be thin. He seems to me to know nothing about men, except their dress, their voice, their buttonholes, their manner of taking meals and furnishing rooms. This rather includes the bulk of moderners. Perhaps I misjudge them: is it that they only represent spirit by flesh, and that men can never do more than hint at soul by such photography? I think not. And *Ibsen*; what of him? I wonder do you know anything of Euripides? and did you ever see Way's verse translation of him, published by Macmillan? You would find a deal of satisfaction and light in the plays, I think. One passage in the Hecuba stays with me. (Though my Greek is small, I have to read in Greek, with, unhappily, only partial appreciation.) Polyxena is to be sacrificed by Pyrrhus Pelides. She tears apart her robe, and stands 'beautiful and like a statue' (as Euripides says: do you question the taste?): then offers him her breast or her throat. He, willing and yet unwilling, spares her breast but strikes her throat. The affecting and gloriously human part is, that, as she falls, she gathers her robe about her, 'lest the rude soldiery should see what it is not fit man should see in a maiden'.

You may well discover much that is questionable in me beside my faltering but still triumphant egoism. I am weak and incapable; perhaps also I am ill-informed; but of one thing I am quite certain. There are and must always be doubts as to what is right or wrong, beautiful or deformed; ideals will always fall short of perfection, or else fail; what we have planned we can never entirely achieve; but one ideal is attainable certainly, and as certainly it is perfect, though confined. If I shall speak ignobly or ludicrously, it is because I am ignoble: my subject is not. I mean private life, and particularly domestic life in whatever family we are placed, whether our own or one of which we are a small part. If we despair of everything else, we need not despair here. And moreover I am not at all sure that there is anywhere a loftier, while there could be no sweeter, perfection than that of a household. I am not sure, either, that many, if not all, would not be wiser to restrict themselves to what is called a narrow sphere of perfection, and use the fancy which they fling so wildly and uselessly elsewhere in a position where no thing that is beautiful can fail. For my part, I only wish that, save in the few cases where interference is inevitable, I could devote myself to thought intended for putting in practice in a sphere no broader than I have described. No doubt I discourse like a family man, or a mere sentimentalist enamoured of board and bed and redfaced 'chickens', but I fancy I speak of something a good deal above their imaginations, even if this gives me no better character than that of the worm who aspires to be an eel but is compelled to remain worm. Another advantage (you will say): egoism here is in its glory, peerless like the yolk in its own egg.

I feel bound to insert, after any and every such sally as this, an apology founded on my very strong doubt that I talk ridiculously; well-intentioned of course, but with an extravagant taste for bathos and no sense of proportion.

I can't help thinking you are too hard upon Matthew Arnold. He is, indeed, as you say, a halfway man, but that is because he is a pioneer if ever there was one. But one thing he does seem to me to want (if I may copy his own wrong judgment of Shelley?), he 'wants matter, a subject matter', and more especially in his prose. He has a very fair flexible style, quite one of the best of his time, and he has a fine sense of shape and proportion: then comes in his lamentable want of premisses. Allowing for these 'terrible wants', as Carlyle says when he pronounces *Charles XII* by Voltaire very fine but 'wanting in truth', there is much to be got from him, I think, if we would only send our own probably inferior individualities to sleep for the time being. As I think I said once before, I have a confidence in implicit obedience, amounting almost to servility; and I would have the majority of men choose their masters and then shut some of their eyes to follow blindly, knowing that after all the more outward eyes have far less work and use than the inward. I believe very much in some sort of content, in creating as it were an atmosphere for a man, wherein he may work out his work in known and fixed placidity. The great objection, people would say, is that this is possible for so few; nay, can be attempted for so few. But that must always be the case with a beginning. I admit, however, that I may here only be applying generally what I find or fancy would be beneficial for me in particular. I see that this placid atmosphere would be good for me, and most adapted for bringing out what there is worthy in me, and immediately spring to a desire that all people should aim at the same position. Yet this need not be wrong; with allowances for the vast space between me and your 'strong men', it maybe I am not far out, and seek just what they seek, to proselytise, to convince, to persuade us of the universality of their own opinions. With you I admit the vanity of attempting to lay down any fixed rules for life; but I do think there are many such rules, which, though utterly different and of varying breadth, if fully followed out, would all lead to truth. It is this completeness that is wanting. People are not prepared to do anything perfectly. All which is so lamentable if we compare it to other ages, many of which had their fixed ideals absorbing the enthusiasm of vast multitudes at one moment; think of chivalry, the Madonna, think of asceticism and the very schoolmen whose language I almost fell into just now ('universality of ideas'). They may not have been divine perfection: but they were perfections: and at any rate how poor our present ideals are, athleticism, literary fame, in comparison. Don't you think so? Or are you smiling contempt-uously to see me writing down the thoughts of others under the persuasion that they are my own? I have red so much that I am always afraid that what I call my knowledge is only a trans-plantation of the knowledge of others; which I fear, although as you see it in part answers that ideal obedience I have spoken of. If you would only blow me up, call me a fool, and a pretentious coxcomb, you would do me a world of good at the expense of only a short annoyance. You think I am 'fishing' perhaps? No: honestly I have no sense at all of my own position, and always tumble toward extreme humility or extreme conceit. Unless you can persuade me I am neither an idiot nor a genius, I shall begin to think you too kind like Helen, and indeed like all I know. They seem in a conspiracy to keep me in the dark about my most interesting self. They often flatter; they never deride; so I frequently go in for a long satire of myself, if I can get an acquaintance tolerant enough to assist: and you will doubtless have the pleasure of hearing me at some time or another; for it is only with those who have sympathy in some degree that I can unburthen myself even in this contorted and diseased fashion.

When you speak of the difficulty of progress and say that 'our millions are still but unreflecting animals' you touch on a subject much too stupendously alarming for any attention, like that of a dilettante. Population! Yes, and I have red about it for what is called political economy.

How affected it was of me to ask you if you tasted that joy of Lucretius! There is my want of balance; to apply a lofty example to something so comparatively insignificant. After all, the stoicism allures me by its magnificence. It is the sublime again,

123

giving that ghastly joy as when I watch one pine on a cold ridge at morning, blackest when the heavens are whitest, one pine and the sound of the sea in a still air.

I will not send you my *Speaker*[3] paper, but will send the next, which ought to appear soon. You would laugh heartily at it, except a partly allegorical passage in which a puppet I introduce to represent myself has a most tragic meeting with the spirit of Nature (pardon me) and falls, 'slain in life by the frost of a great melancholy'; and so on; all very sublime but a little uninteresting to everyone but myself. As a child of 16, I was supposed to have some gift for description; now I have not a particle of descriptive power. In this respect I am an interesting study. Through overelaboration and reading and imitation I have visibly destroyed that power; and what is left I at least can not say: I have designed a long series of Chapters on the same subject of this youth (his name is Basil: I have a little cousin of that name), and hope in time to impose them all on the *Speaker*. It all rests, as you would suppose from that voluble account of my idiosyncrasies, not upon any thought, but upon a possible impressionableness in me, and relies a good deal on mystery or mist. For instance: I lead a youth to a mountain well, into which he looks, finding an infinity in the slender spring; and again he comes in his manhood, to find it deep indeed in reflection of sky and so on, but – bounded and no longer infinite – dead leaves and stones have accumulated, and a bough has crossed the brilliance and made a half shadow. You can guess my intent, and laugh at the ingenious futility of the thing perhaps. And much more of a similar kind. Have I told you this before, and much else in my letter? I hope not. Please tell me if I write too much; if I am too prolix.

Few people have any claims to style in poetry; does Ernest Radford write prose then? Whoever has not studied prose style now, I wonder. Most have far too little time to spare any of it upon what is a kind of luxury. Yet there is some sort of morality in strenuously achieving a nearly perfect style, in building, as the Greeks said, ('build the lofty rhyme') the cottage or the temple of living sounds. Pater is, I am sure, the only example of his own theories. Robert Louis S. is far below him, though he, too, consciously builds. I always think style, in its limited point – the perfect sentence, is like the casting by a spider of its thin thread far out from itself towards some remote object, to attain which is its intent, but to fall short of which by a hair's breadth is to fail utterly.

How sarcastic you are about my saying somewhat 'striking' about books! That is too bad. Poor pretty Sappho: but I will force her upon you some day.

You will never believe I am as busy as I protest, after letters of this length. Yet I write only because I must. I am still very busy. Then please write to me. I am yours full of hope.

Edwy

1 Lucian Oldershaw; see *Edward Thomas: A Portrait* pp. 21–2.
2 ET refers to a change of employment.
3 'Shadows of the Hills', in the ETC, Cardiff.

My dear Harry

I am wondering what you think when we settle down to write at such immense intervals, and hoping you think as I do myself. For what a twiddling of thumbs is letter writing, at least for me! Unless it becomes vanity and says good things. Surely it is a twiddling of thumbs, during the tediousness of absence, with good friends – during the tediousness of intercourse with indifferents. And so I console myself. Yet I can not help somehow regretting I hear so little from you and let you hear so little of myself: you see it is not the 'usual' thing: other people write more often, don't they? But after all I think it is only my selfishness that keeps me from writing more frequently; and I paint to myself your satisfaction, while I am myself rather fretting, without recognising that you are probably the same. Only say you would like me to write oftener – then I will. It is only the motive power that I need, a start. One advantage you have over me: I have nobody to inquire of about you.

How glad I was to have your letter, and on Sunday, too, when I always look for something, and never get it. Several times you have done the same. Yes, let us go into the country all together. Shall it be on Helen's birthday? For I hope I shall be home then. Of course the vac. is long, and begins – oh! – on June 16, but then I am obliged to pay one or two country visits of days or weeks – at Pontardulais, South Wales, at Swindon, possibly also at Clifton.

Does one ever ask any other person's opinion of one's own verses, without secretly believing in them? I don't believe in mine, but I am going to show you four I wrote the other day. I would rather you told me that not only were the words unmusical and the construction prosaic, but the sentiments also not sentiments at all, and the whole uninteresting, – than that you omitted to mention them. Here they are, if I can trust memory:

Weary of April's oversweet
Anemone and marigold –
I turned my feet
To her the meek and bold.

'Let me but speak to thee, or thou
To me unhastily, of naught:
Of love not now,'
I moaned with heart distraught, (!)

Wistfully smiling, then, she stept
To lift me with love's best, though I
Unheeding wept
And cared not to reply.

Ah! when repose came – cruel bliss –
To her sweet toil she turned and wove,
And bitter 'tis (or And would not kiss:
We cannot always love.

'Twas she owned pain I
could not move

I don't know Henley's prose, but his verses are very empty and bad. I should think he could feel well enough: certainly he cannot write of what he feels.

I won't tell you what I have been reading; besides I fancy I do too much, for my head is dull and as if clogged; nor can I get over it by early bed, light meals, and two or three walks a day. Perhaps it is the entire solitude of my life. However, I have looked at Flaubert's letters. These accursed Frenchmen, with their *gout, plaisir, amour, filletes* etc, and the way they end up letters to male friends '*Mille embrassades tendres*' etc etc. Then they talk of having *enormement vecu*, and despise life and the bourgeois. If their philosophy was what it boasted to be, they should see that it is all due to the absurd licence of their *jeunesse triste*, and that licence itself is not at all the fire of nature, but simply habit and novelty and example; once I suppose prostitutes were made because men had inordinate desires: now men have desires because there are prostitutes. If I am wrong, even some of these Frenchmen are very ludicrous in their *tristesse* and *ennui*. I will not be tolerant, even if I am called prudish in revenge. I think, too, Englishmen are not nearly so absurd. These fellows laugh at religion, when it is want of it, or neglect of it, that makes them the asses they are. When do they become men – cease to be boys – in France? At thirty? When Flaubert is engrossed in his art he is proud to say he is serious enough to avoid desire to 'devoiler' etc., when he sits opposite 'aucun jupon'. Yet I heartily like his writing, as writing, and am eager to reach his extravagant precepts on style. It may not be worth our while, some of us may not be fitted, many have not the time, to find the 'mot propre', but there is no question he is right. There is a difference between his writing and Stevenson's mere sweetness and studied curiousness of phrase.

I am impatient to get to Lincoln College. One thing I hope to get there – religion. I find such a need of that, as an informing spirit in all I do and am. If I can be serious enough, I hope to find satisfaction in the Church of England: it will be my fault if I don't. I want, as Milton says in those pathetic closing lines of his Epic, 'a place to rest'.

I am too doubtful about my own writing to think of making an effort towards completing another volume. I shall wait. Perhaps some good will come of rivalry and comparison – if there is any for me – at College. I hope so. I have need of such comparison, otherwise my writing is of a hothouse type.

Goodbye, my dear Harry. I hope all is well.

Edwy

My dear Harry

Thank you for the two poems. You have brought on yourself all these others now.[1] Tell me which you like, if you like any, as I hope you may; and tell me anything that strikes you in reading them, either general or particular. I don't suppose anyone's warning or advice will have any direct active effect. But I want to know an honest reader's opinion because I seem to be committed to a new path that does not promise money and I want any confirmation I can get that it promises at any rate some advance in effectiveness. I had got past poetical prose and my new feeling is that here I can use my experience and what I am and what I know with less hindrance than in prose, less gross notebook stuff and mere description and explanation.

I have begun to write 'Marlborough' now and can do nothing else, but if you and Janet come down any time after this weekend I shall be game for a walk or two, and you can take a stick away.

Yours ever, Edward Thomas

---

1 The following typescript poems accompany this letter: 'Tears', 'The Huxter', 'A Cat', 'Adlestrop', 'Two Pewits', 'July', 'Digging', 'The Path', 'After Rain', 'The Mountain Chapel', 'November', 'The Chalk Pit', 'Beauty', 'The Signpost', 'An Old Song', 'March the Third', 'Interval', 'The Lofty Sky', 'Over the Hills', 'Ambition', 'April', 'Fifty Faggots', 'Song', 'Health', 'But these things also', 'A Gentleman', 'The Penny Whistle', 'The Barn', 'Goodnight', 'The Bridge'.

This is the present order of the typescripts. 'The Huxter' is signed 'Edward Eastaway' in Helen's hand.

My dear Janet,

I have left it too late to write a letter to you and Harry. The pressure has increased and now the day is approaching and it is all I can do to keep level. Worst of all I am afraid I could not help becoming introspective again if I wrote at any length. For my early impressions were far pleasanter than my later. The people are already on my nerves and the shelling is no sort of joy to me. Also yesterday I had a thing to do which I had to give up – to climb the inside of a factory chimney in order to observe from the top. I couldn't or I didn't do it.

Your parcel arrived a week ago and very welcome it was. Everything was good and so was the choice of what to send. Thank you very much. Thank Harry too for his part in the letter but tell him not to joke about leave. There isn't any at all in this Army, except for the sick. So there is only one chance of coming home before the war is over and I don't expect that to be very soon.

We are going to shoot now. This is not an excuse for breaking off. But I have waited day after day for a real opportunity and now I know it won't come. If by chance it should I will not miss it. Will you please do the same or more?

Give my love to Harry and the girls and to Jones and Mrs Jones. I hope we are going to meet and walk again.

Ever yours,
Edward Thomas